# Jeff, One Lonely Guy

Published by Amazon Publishing
P.O. Box 400818
Las Vegas, NV 89140

ISBN-13: 9781612183244
ISBN-10: 1612183247

# Jeff, One Lonely Guy

Jeff Ragsdale, David Shields, Michael Logan

**amazon**publishing

# Introduction

In late October 2011, my friend and former student Jeff Ragsdale posted this flyer around New York City:

Jeff recently realized he had sabotaged his stand-up and acting careers. He was down and out, living in a tiny room in a boarding house in Harlem. Having gone through a painful breakup this fall, he was extremely lonely. "New York is a terribly difficult place to meet people," he wrote me. "I was isolated. I wanted to talk to as many people as I could, but not through a keyboard. I wanted to hear a voice, so I came up with the idea of posting this flyer around NYC."

Jeff thought he'd get a handful of phone calls. He received approximately a hundred calls and texts the first day. The second day he started hearing from people out of state. Several posted a picture of his flyer on the article- and image-sharing site reddit.com, where it quickly became an internet sensation. Soon he began receiving around 700 calls and 1,000 texts each day.

He's spoken with people from all over and as far away as Spain, Switzerland, Saudi Arabia, Iraq, Taiwan, Australia. Thousands of people have written blogs about the flyer. He's received more than 60,000 phone calls and texts.

I was, to say the least, intrigued when he told me about some of the remarkably urgent and candid phone calls and texts he'd received; we quickly realized there was the potential here for an unusual book. Over the next two months, Jeff sent me thousands of texts he received and hundreds of pages of phone conversations that he wrote up from notes. Michael Logan and I rearranged the material into a chorus of voices talking about the searing loneliness of existence in America at this moment.

People reveal remarkable things to Jeff. Many formerly abused and abandoned women call him. A 16-year-old who survived ovarian cancer and chemo writes Jeff in order to feel a connection to the outside world again. Air Force pilots stationed overseas send pictures of themselves dressed as clowns for Halloween and give Jeff advice on how to deal with women. A Starbucks "associate" texts him that she doesn't have the courage to quit her job because she needs the money, though this thought makes her angry. A premed student says he's happy that Jeff put up his flyer because it forces him to think about his issues before dealing with patients. A pimp texts to find out how Jeff is doing with the ladies.

And Jeff reveals remarkable things to the people who call, and to us. It's definitely a two-way mirror: Jeff gives at least as much as he gets.

Mikhail Lermontov said about his own book, *A Hero of Our Time*, the first Russian novel, "Some were dreadfully insulted, and quite seriously, to have held up as a model such an immoral character as my protagonist, Pechorin; others shrewdly noticed that the author had portrayed himself and his acquaintances. *A Hero of Our Time* is in fact a portrait, but not of an individual; it is the aggregate of the vices of our whole generation in their fullest expression."

I think of Jeff and the people portrayed here in the same way. This is Dostoevsky's *Notes from Underground* told by and for and in the digital age. This is the authentic sound of human beings, at ground level, often in economic freefall, trying to connect in whatever way possible, below the radar of Big Media. This is Occupy Loneliness. This is America singing—singing a dirge.

**David Shields**
March 2012

**A note on formatting:** Names without phone numbers indicate blocked calls. Ellipses within a passage represent the deletion of Jeff's responses in a phone conversation or text exchange. Transcribing phone conversations, we conformed to standard American usage; we didn't correct text lingo. The passages written by Jeff are in italics.

# I. Posting a Flyer

**If anyone wants
to talk about
anything,
call me**

**(347) 469-3173.**

**—Jeff, one lonely guy**

**570-231-XXXX**
So how did everyone get your number in the first place?

**516-859-XXXX**
Wow, I just saw your sign on a pole a couple days ago.

**478-213-XXXX**
Flyer guy?

**347-441-XXXX**

Jeff, can I call you?

**970-433-XXXX**

Sup :)

**646-785-XXXX**

Why did you post this sign?

**908-420-XXXX**

Im lonely too.

**361-688-XXXX**

Jeff, are you real?

**843-330-XXXX**

What's your gamer tag?

**Rodrigo**

I definitely feel disconnected. Too virtual.

**980-328-XXXX**

Jeff, you intrigue me. I hope I can talk to you more in depth.

**270-604-XXXX**

Whose number is this?

**347-638-XXXX**

Wow, this is a real number.

**Lydia**

No, we haven't met. I saw your flyer and it would be cool to get to know you. How are you?

**910-818-XXXX**

Talk to me....Suckish and lonely.Wbu?

**908-420-XXXX**

Standing out in the cold :(...Talk to me.

**605-321-XXXX**

Jeffy poo

**Lucinda**

Hey, Jeff, I saw your number on a phone pole and decided to text you.

**646-734-XXXX**

Keep me company.

**Brittany (210-323-XXXX)**

Hello Lonely Man. One question—whatever possessed you to post your number up for the world to see?

*It's kind of a self-portrait.*

## 917-886-XXXX

I dnt need to tlk i was calling cause i saw ur poster whats the deal with that?... Dude i don't know u and my friend tld me to call u as a joke....Plz like im fine idk u plz stop....No offense but i feel weird and like yeah sorry to come off mean but plz feel better and get better.

## 718-530-XXXX

I hate myself too. You know those ads that are like "Would you have a drink with you?" To be totally honest, I absolutely wouldn't.

## 908-420-XXXX

I saw your ad and I just wanted to talk for awhile.

## Caitlin (409-350-XXXX)

Was Kira the one that started all of this?

## 219-688-XXXX

Hey is this Jeff? I just called you to see if it was for real, but I chickened out and couldn't talk.

## 646-533-XXXX

Yo, bro, u gonna leave me and my balls hangin dry? Why put up the ad if ur not gonna reply?

## 917-361-XXXX

She won't ever talk to you again?

**917-373-XXXX**

Jeff, I saw your thingy-ma-bobber and—oh, wait, I can't talk to you.


**Erin**

Jeff, we should be friends. That way you won't be lonely anymore....
Aw well thank you. I'm here for you. Just so you know.


**847-668-XXXX**

Hi. I read your poster. And wondered if you'd like a new friend?


**602-206-XXXX**

I find your experiment inspiring! I just called you a little while ago.


**646-641-XXXX**

I saw your number in Chelsea. I work in the area. How are you,
lonely guy?


**Caitlin**

I'm good. I'm always good.


*Caitlin told me she's bipolar, terribly depressed, and nearly
committed suicide last year.*


**949-572-XXXX**

My son introduced me to Imgur.com. It's great to see your flyer.
Jeff, what you did took courage. I like it. It showed trust of humanity.
You not lonely anymore?

**Mike, from Brooklyn**

I found your number on 4chan. Bro, you from Brooklyn?

*I told Mike I live in a boarding house in West Harlem. Trash covers the sidewalks. The awnings are rusted; the signs are torn. Old men stand on the streets all day, bullshitting. They play dominoes and cards at night. A man was shot in front of the boarding house where I live. Every block: drug dealers on all corners, check-cashing places, Chinese takeout. After one a.m., every question is, "What do you need—weed, coke, heroin?"*

**Hans**

Hey, Jeff. I was figuring to see if I'd be the longest-distance person you've had....I'm in Korea.

**Mel**

Hey jeff i called from Japan and you didn't answer, way to waste my minutes ass!

**912-656-XXXX**

Hey. I'm in Georgia. Hey, do you know my sister, Barbara, by chance?... I guess it is a big city.

**209-914-XXXX**

Has hella people texted you?

**917-520-XXXX**
There are so many people in Manhattan, but it can be the loneliest place on earth. I lived in Beirut and it was a beautiful place. Less lonely than Manhattan, actually.

**212-203-XXXX**
Hey hottie. How's Dallas?

**970-433-XXXX**
Jeff! It's the people who just called you from Colorado! Wassup?

**Marta, 50s, woman from Ecuador (917-385-XXXX)**
I was walking down 5th Avenue and saw your flyer. I'm incredibly lonely, too. I'm the "lonely woman." No family, friends. I live in a tiny room of a shared apartment in Queens. You want to go for a walk next weekend?

*I said yes.*

**713-478-XXXX**
Are you the guy from New York?

**Miguel, Miami**
Love your poster. Mind if I try it in Miami?... Thanks, Jeff....Come on down. I'll hook you up with clubs and chicks.

**Sanitation worker (917-359-XXXX)**
Jeff, is it you who's been posting those flyers? We can fine you.

### American man in Saudi Arabia

I saw it because somebody posted your flyer on my Facebook page....No, it's cool....You can be lonely in the desert or at Times Square.

### Loralei, San Diego

Saw your flyer. I've been in San Diego for the last 30 years and I just wanted to talk to a New Yorker who's doing something bold. Let's get together.

### Kerry, Sydney, Australia (011-614-XXXX-XXXX)

Hey Jeff—are you still lonely? Or cursing the day you posted that flyer? Sadly, loneliness is a terrible side effect of a connected virtual world.

### 310-662-XXXX

You rule reddit, Jeff.

### 347-364-XXXX

Wassrong with you? Y u got problems??

*I'm a self-saboteur. Growing up, I was told over and over I'd never amount to anything; when I actually get some success, I can't deal with it. I don't think I deserve it, so I destroy it. I know that's what happened with my stand-up comedy career. I was one of the best storytelling stand-ups in New York. I did really well on NBC's* Last Comic Standing. *Then it was gone. I'm ashamed to even show up now to stand-up gigs.*

**806-223-XXXX**

Sounds fun. Better than Arkansas.

**787-518-XXXX**

I'm pretty sure you'll find someone thanks to the sign.

*A woman saw me putting up a sign on the street and called me that night. She sends me dozens of texts every day. Has a grad degree in social work. Says she's a virgin at 26. She's not bad looking. Says she "jerks off a lot," though. She's only kissed guys, and not for three years. Last guy she was with was from Germany and he went back. Her texts are all about love. When I met her on the street, she had a strange, smiling look in her eyes. My intuition says to stay away. When I first met Kira, my intuition said the same thing.*

**568-894-XXXX**

Pick up!!!!!!!! I need you!!!!!!!!

**Damian**

Ur creepy.

**406-205-XXXX**

Think we'll ever meet?

**917-762-XXXX**

Hey, are you a pedo or a creeper? I guess a pedo wouldn't put up a flyer. He'd just be doing pedo stuff. What about a creeper?

**Jenna, Memphis (901-568-XXXX)**

Maybe you should put your photo on your flyer? I'm still trying to stalk/find u on Facebook.

**20-year-old woman, student, Eugene, Oregon**

Saw your flyer on Facebook. I'm doing environmental studies. The comments said you were a really nice person.

> *A woman saw my sign on Houston Street and called. We had a nice chat. I told her I've met a few women in person who responded to my flyer. She said, "Any girl who calls a guy from a street sign and meets up with him wants to get raped."*

**Betsy**

I love this flyer. Is it weird that I love this?… It's also true I once went on a Craigslist date with a total stranger because it was his birthday and he had no one to celebrate with… So maybe it's not weird that I love this.

**702-782-XXXX**

Lol. Just saw ur # on a window. Just want to know y u put it up for?

> *Today I'm meeting Amy, who said on the phone that she and her colleague saw my poster and wanted to see who would talk to me first.*

**Katie**

Hi Jeff! I heard you're one cool cat. Guess you aren't lonely anymore, huh?… That's amazing. I may put some flyers up in Baltimore and see what happens. Any lasting connections from it?

**Kira (6 weeks ago)**
You ruined my life.

**409-422-XXXX**
Feel free to text back this random girl when you're awake.

**347-452-XXXX**
Hey Jeff. My name is Cameron....I'm an 18-year-old awesome homosexual freshman at City University. I saw your advertisement and it made me laugh my fucking ass off....Why so lonely, buddy?

**Drunk woman, 4 a.m., looking at my flyer at 14th and 6th**
My boyfriend is going to break up with me unless I shave my vagina. What do you think?... I think it's shallow too. I'm going to call you back.

*The drunk woman never called back.*

**224-441-XXXX**
It's an interesting idea. I've never seen anyone do that with a flyer.

**818-281-XXXX**
Wait—who is this?... This doesn't sound like you....What flyer?... How old are you?

**706-326-XXXX**
I saw what you posted. Thought I'd send you a text and say your sign worked.

**Krystal, 17 (319-545-XXXX)**
Hey you're really cute, just saying.

**584-246-XXXX**
Someone should give you a present.

**Sara**
Have you ever had one-night stands?

**Mark**
Hey hot stuff!

**636-544-XXXX**
You're semi-famous.

**Kelly, 28, bartender, NYC**
Loved the flyer. You never know who's calling ya. It's like a surreal movie.

**917-544-XXXX**
Holy shit! Are you famous?

**Jason**
U stole the show on imgur—200K hits in 10 minutes.

**647-547-XXXX**
U r famous. Take me to a hotel and fuck me.

**512-569-XXXX**

Random girl I know sent that when I gave her my phone. Disregard...This is the chick that took the phone. *(Sends picture: she's pretty hot.)*... Just out of curiosity, how old are you?... Women be hijacking my phone....Prepare to be pestered.

**Ashley (938-574-XXXX)**

I'm sure you're excellent. Mmm. I'd eat you up.

**210-382-XXXX**

Ur helping others with ur flyer.

**Ashley**

That's quite flattering. I'd ride you crazy. I would love to have you inside me someday.

**Matt, Columbus (614-843-XXXX)**

This's killer. I wish I did it. You must get tons of ladies. Shout out for the ladies.

**Arizona girl**

Hey its the chick from Arizona. You must get a shit ton of people calling.

*I know I should have left the relationship. We both should have. I hit Kira in the face once, but it's not as simple as it sounds.*

**954-990-XXXX**

I know how that is....Why did it end?... Do you regret it?... What you're doing is an interesting way to get over tough times.

**Kathleen**

Hi, is this Jeff, and was your sign posted in Union Square true? How are you doing now? I was really touched by your flyer. I understand all about tough breakups. I just wanted to tell you that you are deeply loved. If you still need to talk, I'd love to encourage you. Otherwise, have a very blessed day!

*All true, but this stuff's much easier said than done. There's a lot about me not to love.*

**Ella, 16 (636-544-XXXX)**

Hi Jeff. Your flyer means more to me than just some guy that wants someone to talk to. To me it means that someone cares. Someone wants to know. I just wanted to let you know that your interest in my story and my poetry means so much to me. I've gone through a lot and when someone takes time to say they're interested, it means a lot. Thank you.

**Nathan**

How it feel to be the most famous pedophile on the net, Jeff? A million searches for ur flyer.

**307-640-XXXX**

I just saw your ad on break.com and I just wanted to tell you to quit being a fag.

**307-349-XXXX**
So tell me about yourself, man.

**Kevin, 36, Brooklyn**
I could never post a flyer like yours. I'm too sensitive. They diagnosed me bipolar, but I don't believe bipolarism exists. Some people are just born with more emotions and sensitivity than others, and it has made my life extremely difficult....I don't have many friends. I spend most of my time in my apartment.

**James**
Saw your flyer. Has it come to that level of lonely? I'm not making fun of you, man, just curious about other human experiences. I am not looking for any weird hook-ups....Really? Other shy folk, looking for a buddy?

**Erica, 26 (917-691-XXXX)**
Did you ever wish on eyelashes?

**Jennifer (212-775-XXXX)**
Posters were not a bad idea. I'm Jennifer, by the way.

*I remember that first punch. It started when I grabbed Kira's leg. She sat up and punched me as hard as she could in the face. I actually saw stars. Kira's superhumanly strong. Her whole family is. Things spiraled out of control after that. It was as if we both lost respect. Our roommates were scared. They could hear us yelling and fighting. They even slipped an eviction note under our door: "We've never been around this type of violence. It's frightening. We know you're not preparing for acting gigs, like you say." They knew Kira and I were actors. After our first loud fight, Kira told them we were rehearsing for an audition. I think they bought it the first couple times.*

**646-246-XXXX**

Wow that's a lot of responses in a month! That's awesome! Did you just decide to do it for yourself or was it an experiment?

**847-770-XXXX**

Oh, I expected this number to be fake.

**Marsha (914-536-XXXX)**

Question: is it smart to go for a degree, then pursue a career in acting? Or should I just go for it?

**786-970-XXXX**

Yo, you like Star Wars?

**Ray**

You are famous. I'm nobody. Who are you? Are you nobody too? No, you're famous, asshole. I live in a box. Buy me a car.

**315-214-XXXX**

A friend of mine informed me that Ashton Kutcher saw the signs too and tweeted a picture of one. Maybe he sent a call or text your way!

**910-336-XXXX**

I just wanted to talk to somebody right now. Where'd you go?

**Wealthy Hamptons woman**

I'm in Manhattan, looking at cars and having some drinks....Your flyer was fabulously interesting....I've got many gorgeous women to set you up with.

**Woman with thick, old-money British accent**

Jeffrey, darling. It's Emma. We met the other evening. *(Have never met her.)* I saw your flyer. I'm perturbed that you're still advertising yourself this way. I don't think you quite need it. We hit it off rather smashingly. I'll ring you back, dear.

**Donna**

I just flew in from LA and was in a bad mood, then I saw your sign on the street....Ha! I cast reality shows.

**Victoria**

Hi Jeff. It's Victoria from FM News 101.9. Please call me at 212-363-XXXX....Oops! I gave you the wrong number. It's 212-362-XXXX.

**Tony**

You look a little like Keanu Reeves....Maybe you are Keanu Reeves—doing research for a film about a lonely guy who puts his number on the internet?

**Patrick**

Leave me a voicemail. Can't talk, but wanna hear your voice.

**April (989-450-XXXX)**

Hi Jeff—Brian Quinn sent me....I'm doing all right with the exception that I just broke a lamp....Are you going to be on Quinn's show?

**Rob**

This is Rob from Queens. I'm a flamboyant dancer in snappy attire. I've been on shows I'm sure you've seen. Shyness has degenerated my life. I can't communicate with people. I'm lonely because I'm in a shell. I'm not working now. I get money from New York state because I'm mentally different. I saw your flyer. I'll call you tomorrow, in the a.m., ok?

**Meldi (832-729-XXXX)**

I'm acting in a show right now at intermission. I'll text you later. Sorry!

**Tom**

Some things happen arbitrarily....I worked in finance and met this big-time movie producer at a party and now he's getting me parts in films....Keep me posted on how your flyer works out for you...

**Jacqueline**

You are the Tom Cruise of the web.

**Connor**

You're Tumblr famous!

**512-569-XXXX**

How is your 15 minutes of fame?

**Cath**

Do you regret posting your #? You're fuckin' VIRAL baby!

*I'd been recognized a few times on the streets of New York when I did stand-up. It always felt wonderful, especially when I was with people. I'd brush off the recognition, like, "Oh, thanks. I was ok, not that good." But now that I've put my "Lonely Jeff" flyer up and it's gone viral, I'm getting thousands of phone calls and texts a day. I know this bubble will burst, but it's amazing. I embrace it—just the fact that people are interested in me, want to talk to me. I try to respond to every call and text. Some days I'm on the phone 16 hours. When I sit in Starbucks and my phone rings nonstop, I feel important. I know it's shallow, but it feels great to be wanted. The irony of the situation is the second my internet "fame" kicked in, I got a call from Detective Alvarez of the NYPD, telling me he had a warrant for my arrest, regarding harassing emails to Kira, my ex. On the one hand, I felt phenomenal. On the other, I felt as if my life were coming to an end.*

**Nancy**

My phone's about to black out. I will call u when its charged.

**347-620-XXXX**

I'm not feeling well but I'll get better. Is this Jeff?

*I had a woman from Spokane on the phone who was in the process of committing suicide. God knows why she would've called me after seeing my flyer on imgur.com. She tried to kill herself once before by ingesting over 100 pills. She was doing the same thing this time: ingesting. I had her call 1-800-SUICIDE.*

### Belinda

I think that's an interesting way to reach out. Hope you're having a great night.

### Sandra, Boise

Hey Jeff!!... I'm a good listener and an awesome friend to anyone who needs one. I'm also incredibly strange....I might just do that, Jeff. I'm having a hard time right now....It's nice to know there's someone out there who gives his time to talk to strangers...You're a good person. I can tell. I'm not so good....My life just kind of fell apart in a blink of an eye. Things were so incredibly good there for a while....I tell people's fortunes for a living.

### Maria (561-386-XXXX)

Well, without too much elaboration, let's just say things could be better.

### Woman visiting NYC from London

I saw your flyer on the street and just called to say hello....I understand the difficulties of life and loneliness....What are you going to be for Halloween?

**Three teens from Fresno**

Jeff, we loved your poster, but you should've put a zombie on it, dude....We're watching a zombie video and hanging out.

**202-477-XXXX**

Is Funny Pics ur bitch? U own it.

**717-816-XXXX**

I called to see what the story was.

**917-301-XXXX**

We live in a disconnected society....Did you think up this idea while you were smoking a blunt?

**Kori, Cincinnati**

One lonely guy. One lonely country.

**Office workers in Switzerland**

We saw your flyer on Facebook. It's hysterical. How did you come up with the idea, mate?

**Jason, Columbus (419-252-XXXX)**

You had one of those rare moments of clarity that we get once or twice in our lives.

**Middle-aged man, Rocky Mountains (414-430-XXXX)**

Your flyer was rather absorbing....I come from a sales back-ground....Having a Bloody Mary, hooking up with my fiancée to catch some football later....Can my sales team contact you for a strategic marketing phone call?... Great!

**Loretta**
How's the random text biz been, Tiger?

**305-773-XXXX**
It's like free therapy.

**704-712-XXXX**
Have fun answering phone calls for the rest of your life.

**602-330-XXXX**
You should've been a marketing major.

*An advertising exec talked about the loneliness of America. He wants to build a house where people can go to "just talk." It would be called the "Happy House."*

**Geddy, Chicago (847-924-XXXX)**
Aren't you sick of talking to people?

**646-884-XXXX**
Why do you think relationships are so tough?

**Mary Beth**
This is Mary Beth saying hi. I liked your flyer. Please don't call me back.

**805-407-XXXX**

This is epic.

**212-280-XXXX**

I'm calling about the computer sale.

# II. Notes on Childhood

*Both of my parents had children from previous marriages. Mom was 40 when she had Martin. He was an accident, and to keep the accident occupied, 13 months later they had me, the playmate for the accident. They actually called me that, the playmate. Cindy, my stepsister, told me years later that Mom drank basically every night when I was in her. I know I have fetal alcohol syndrome. It's similar to Down syndrome, the way it slants your eyes. I have these Asiany eyes. Both my parents had big round WASPy eyes. I have this thin upper lip too—another sign.*

**850-348-XXXX**
Birthday: the day your suffering begins.

**Erica**
What else do you want to do to me?

**Single mother, 25, Pittsburgh**
I'm very happy with what you're doing. Many people feel the same way.

**Amy, single mother of 8-year-old boy**

My son's a real handful with me working and everything. I've been married twice, but there's no man in the house now. The truth is I'm a swinger. I like orgies, that kind of stuff.

*I told Amy I'd like to meet up. Before getting married, when my parents were having their affair, they hooked up in a dive motel. Dad's then wife, Carole, came to the room with Dad's daughters. Carole knocked on the door. My parents didn't answer. Carole went to the car and came back with Dad's golf clubs. She broke the window, smashed up the door. Dad's daughters watched in horror as the police arrested their mom.*

**847-417-XXXX**

I grew up in a bipolar family. I'm a forensic psych student from Evanston. I work at a sex shop and petting zoo. Such a pleasure to meet you!

*I saw so many different moods in Kira I started thinking she might be schizophrenic. It scared me how different she was immediately after a fight, becoming another person—an innocent young girl with no cares in the world. And she'd constantly joke, as if we hadn't just fought. I was thinking this must be a defense mechanism for something that went on when she was a child. I know her parents fought a lot. Her dad has a bad temper, and Kira's mom divorced him and ended up going off with a woman.*

**Kira (3 months ago)**

Heathcliff its me Catherine!

*You're a genius, Kira, but to me you will always be Lolita.
Lo-Lee-Ta. You are Lo in the morning. Dolores on the dot-
ted line, but in my arms, Kira, you are always Lo-Leeeeee-
Ta. Light of my life, fire of my loins. My sin, my soul!*

**Kira**

Did you just make that up?

**Jeanine**

My parents don't know I'm a lesbian. If they did, I couldn't see my
girlfriend. I'm just trying to get through high school so I can move in
with my girlfriend. Plus my dad has a bad temper.

*During drunken rages, Dad would throw Mom's clothes off
the deck into the swimming pool. The neighbors could see.
I remember watching the police cuff him to the deck.*

**Erica**

One day it seemed like it just flipped. And everyone seemed like
they just hated me and I hated myself....The result of my childhood
was a confused adult not knowing what to do with life.

**Carola**

My childhood was similar to urs....Strange. Lonely...I was born
an adult and then there were certain experiences where I felt my

childhood-self die. Have you too had those experiences?... Some things you see, life is never the same....I was a beastly little kid.

**605-321-XXXX**
Do you have kids, Jeff?

*Kira said she got picked on often by her family. Her dad, brother, and sister would all make fun of her at dinner. Little jokes, but Kira said they still hurt. They'd make fun of her because she was different. She played by herself. She'd go off in the woods and invent her own games. I can understand the young persona she takes on when she feels tremendous pressure. It's an escape. She'd create imaginary friends.*

**Roberta, Reno (661-371-XXXX)**
I'm a nurse. My kids show me how amazing I am.

**306-280-XXXX**
If you were a tree, what kind of tree would you be, Jeff?

**Alicia, 20, Ohio (937-732-XXXX)**
I love to paint trees and monsters of every imaginable shape and size....I've been chronically shy my whole life. I even quit high school because I was so shy. I went to a doctor who told me I needed to get freaky and weird. I dyed my hair six different colors....I go up to strangers on the street and act like I know them. It's a strange kind of acting, becoming another person, but it helps with shyness....Me and my mom live in this small hippie mecca. We were homeless for a

while because my dad took all the family money when I was 4 and left us. Ten years later he came back and beat up my mom....He's a crazy man, a coke and crack addict, so we moved here to escape him.

*Mom's friends told her to wait until Dad was passed out and then hit him over the head with a frying pan.*

## Chelsea, 18, Denver

I recently got married, but he won't listen, like he only says what he likes, not what I might like, so like if I bring up *Harry Potter*, because I like *Harry Potter* a lot, he rips it apart.

## Betty (631-404-XXXX)

If you don't think I exist, then piss off. If you're going to call me a leech, then leave me alone. And if you think I'm only 16, then so be it. So be it, Lonely Jeff! Piss off!

## Luanne

Forgiveness frees up so much energy. Jeff, you have to forgive everyone in your life to truly live....I'm the cause of all my problems. I grew up in foster homes. I'm terrified of being abandoned.

## 303-217-XXXX

Seeing my dad for the first time in months before he leaves again. You?

## Felicia, 15 (845-464-XXXX)

I wanted to tell you how happy I am after adopting a shelter cat last week. His name is Aleister, after Aleister Crowley.

*Felicia sent me a picture message of Aleister, a white cat
with a black bowtie.*

## Maya

I tried to commit suicide, but my parents called in the middle of it. An
ambulance and the cops came. I'd taken 100 pills. He wasn't even
a boyfriend. My parents said I'd never have a man because I'm so
ugly. I'm from the ugly tree. I love stray cats. I was abused as a child
and now I've lost custody of my boy.

*Mom was habitually abandoned. When her parents would
surface, she'd have to sit in the car while they barhopped.
She watched her parents fight violently. My mom fought
violently with Dad. She even pulled a gun on him one morning after he beat her up the night before.*

## Melissa, archeology major in New Mexico, from Arizona (480-751-XXXX)

Pow. Right in the head. Aunt Stacy's in prison for murder. She
killed her ex with a gun. My grandmother beat my mother as soon
as she started dating. Grandma was jealous, wanted her all to
herself.

*Leslie, my first serious relationship, came home with a hick-
ey on her arm. She said she gave it to herself because she
was bored. At three a.m. I ended up kicking her out of my
room, where she was staying. She never gave me a sense
of security. I was jealous, always thought she was cheating.
Two days later I begged her to take me back.*

**Anitchka, Ukrainian, 20, college student (646-353-XXXX)**
My father was murdered before I was born. I moved to the U.S. at age 3, rebelled majorly as a teen. I had to go to a high school for addicts for a few years upstate....My mother's a hairdresser. My mom and her grandparents want to move back to Kiev because the American dream isn't what they thought it would be....I want to be a veterinarian.

*I met Anitchka at Starbucks at Astor Place. I cried when she explained how her dad got killed. Partly because I was hung over. When I'm hung over, my emotions are out of control.*

**Krystal**
You promise not to forget me?

**Ruben, 29, Colombian**
Pablo Escobar had a hit out on my father, who was a Communist. My father fought against Escobar and got political asylum in the U.S.

**19-year-old forensic psychology student, Brooklyn**
My stepdad was convicted of murder when I was 12. It was on the front page of newspapers and it was surreal. I wrote him a few times and then stopped. I haven't communicated with him for 6 years....You know, people that come from difficult childhoods usually become extremists. They hardly ever gravitate toward the middle. They're way on each side of the spectrum.

*I'm getting a lot of calls from forensic psych students.*

## Girl, 14, Phoenix

I've been beat up many times in my hood....It's ok....Thank you—I try to be...I want to be happy in life. So I think happy....Jeff, you need to move out of NYC to raise a family.

## Young woman, college student, Missouri (913-205-XXXX)

I had a miserable childhood. Nobody helped me. The people who need help most don't get help. My dad abandoned us when I was a baby. He Facebooked me after 20 years and I've been talking to him.

*I can't handle change. This comes from growing up in instability. My parents were raging, violent alcoholics. I crave normality because I've never had it. I just want one more chance with Kira, even though I know she's not good for me, even though I know she'll destroy me and my so-called career.*

## Amy

I'm a case worker for CPS, taking care of children who have been abused. I go to their homes, or foster homes, and feed the kids and take them to school. It can be tough because the mothers often think I'm in the way, but I've been appointed by the state to make sure the children get fed and get to school on time....I need to take some time off, though. I hate where my son and I live right now. I need to find a better place for both of us....There's a sex party happening on Saturday, if you're interested.

**347-376-XXXX**

Hows your counseling from the anger management thing?

**Anya, 13, Delaware (302-653-XXXX)**

I had counseling because my mom found out I was cutting myself. Please don't tell anyone....Smiling makes you live longer....I'm better than I was in the past so I'm really good....In the beginning I got molested by my older stepbrother. I never told anybody for 4 to 5 years. He also rapidly hit my head against a wall and had 2 knives, 1 on me and 1 on my mom....I will but he lives in New Hampshire so I don't think I'll ever see him again....Will you be my friend?... I am—it's just that I don't have a lot of friends. I'm not good at making friends or normal things people do everyday....Yeah without the bad you wouldn't appreciate the good....Have you ever felt like no matter what you do it will never be right?... Have you ever seen Paranormal Activity 1 & 2?

> *My first memory is of my parents rolling on the floor, punching each other's faces, my mom's teeth clenched. The police were always at our house. At one point, my parents were friends with an alcoholic sheriff. When the police would show up, Sheriff Morgan would drive over and smooth things out, talk the police out of hauling Dad to jail.*

**Mitchell**

My dad was diagnosed as a schizophrenic later in life. He was also bipolar. He'd have incredibly robust outbursts and break things at home. He held hundreds of jobs, but couldn't keep any of them. He always thought his coworkers were talking and plotting against him.

He was always the nice, gregarious guy outside our house. The life of the party. No one would believe that he was this violent crazy person until he went to jail.

*A forensic psychologist drilled me about my relationship with Kira. When I finally told her that both Kira and I would lose control and say things we didn't mean in fights, she hung up. She only wanted to hear that I hit Kira.*

**Erica**
Everyone just hurts me.

**636-209-XXXX**
That's why we called! We understand....My friend with phat ass stopped by....I'm sad!... You got my number. I'm lone lonely girl.... Yes, I'd fuck you till the sun came up....I had 2 guys at once twice.... But I like pussy too, so we need 2 girls too....I would love to be with me too!... I might just think of you tonight while I play with myself beside my boyfriend....You think you can handle me?... Fuck me outside your ex's window. Then I'll punch her.

**Erica**
I need a boyfriend that doesn't want me to stay anorexic. I need a family that actually cares, minus the red tape. I need maturity. And I have Xanax. I don't want to have to need anything. I don't. I just want to disappear.

*Kira's dad was depressed most of her childhood. After his business failed, he couldn't do anything but eat and watch*

*TV. He'd sneak out at two in the morning for doughnuts and gained over 100 pounds. He started sleeping downstairs in the basement. Nothing interested him anymore. Kira's mom, Eunice, tried vigorously to keep the marriage together for the kids. Years of counseling. She tried to get him out of the house, but he wouldn't even go for walks with her. Kira would say to her mom, "Can't you please just be nice to Dad and be happy again?" Kira went to one of the last counseling sessions. The counselor asked her mom if she still loved her husband. "No." Eunice suffered from her own bouts of depression. Eunice grew up in a precarious environment herself. Her mother was constantly hospitalized for mania, would go on manic shopping sprees, drink to excess, get into traffic accidents, and disappear for days.*

**Theo (469-237-XXXX)**
My parents argue about everything....How do I ask people out?... What if she says no?... My mom just lost her job.

**Alena, 25**
My dad abandoned me at birth and my mom died when I was 4. I've got an older brother dying of AIDS. My younger sister lives in a homeless shelter and has 3 children by 3 different men, but I have a pretty solid job and rent an apartment.

**Psychologist from Maine**
Did you resent Kira moving in with no money? Did you resent that Kira didn't work? Could she have held a job in her condition?

**512-569-XXXX**

I try really hard, but sometimes I get too much pressure and just cry in the bathroom....Silly females again.

**16-year-old girl, North Carolina**

No, I'm not happy....High school kids think I'm mean....What would make me happy? That's easy. A 16 yr old girl wants drugs to make her happy.

**Alicia**

I'm an addict just like my mom and dad. I was in a terrible relationship where I got beat all the time and was drinking from morning until night. It was completely dysfunctional. I slowed way down after it broke up violently. I still love a party of weed and booze. If I can just binge on weekends, I think I've got it under control. I need to commit to myself for a while before committing to another relationship.

*I started taking Adderall with Kira. I'm an addict, so it was incredibly stupid. I get addicted to anything instantly. I loved Adderall. It was similar to coke. I'd feel warm and happy and upbeat. I'd want more and more. I talk a lot better when I'm on coke or Adderall. The shyness goes away. It makes me want to connect with people.*

**Amy**

I hire a sweet old lady to babysit my son and then I put a strap on and do men I meet at sex parties....It usually goes on in locked rooms and takes the guy months before he'll open up with me....

Men like it but feel embarrassed about liking it....My friend and me are a tandem. She doesn't speak English, so whoever the guy is, he needs to know some Spanish or he's going to freak out at this screaming Spanish woman. She likes to spank people while I watch. Sometimes she likes to walk on a man's back, yelling at him, before giving him a blow job and swallowing.... *(I ask if her friend does intercourse.)*....No, she has a husband.

### 646-943-XXXX

I don't want you unconsciously dumping your baggage on me....I know you are sick....You stink of hurt....I don't want to have sex with you....Your delivery is intense.

### Kira

You are acting like a robot who doesn't have any emotions.

> *I asked a therapist once if I could be a sociopath. She said no, a sociopath would never ask that question. I know I've manipulated people, but I also get filled with tremendous guilt. I've wondered, though, what if my guilt's just from being raised Catholic? Catholicism makes everyone feel guilty. The more I think about it, though, I'm too empathetic to be a sociopath. The only way I can deal sometimes is to just desensitize.*

### Nicole, college student, Oklahoma City

My godfather, who was very close to me, committed suicide last year. It came out of nowhere....My mom works for Halliburton overseas. I see her once a year....My dad's a dick. I don't talk to him....

My deity is the universe. If I died, I'd probably be content. On further introspection, I probably wouldn't....He'd been fighting with his wife. She left with the kids for the weekend, came back, and he had shot himself in the bedroom.

### Kira

Do not try to manipulate me with you having no family. I am dealing with all this and have been for a long time, without family.

*Kira and I were with a tranny in a hotel on West 145th that rents rooms by the hour. First thing the tranny did was take off her shirt and talk about estrogen injections and how even her nipples have been augmented. They were robust nipples. The tranny hasn't had the lower surgery yet, so she tucks it back. She said her name's Mariah—I presume after Mariah Carey. Mariah dreams of one day becoming a pop sensation. The problem is Mariah's afraid to sing. She told us she was abused by an uncle as a child. We found a dealer in the hallway (the halls were creeping with dealers). He said coke would take a few minutes, since it was coming from downtown, but that he had crack. The hotel smelled identical to those little porn booths in XXX stores: bleach and Pine-Sol.*

### Ashley

I imagine you're the kind of man who smells wonderful. I want to nuzzle you and smell you. Nothing turns me on more than smell.

*I remember Dad saying to Mom, "This room smells like BO." He was pointing to the guest bedroom. At 11, I knew*

*exactly what he meant, that Mom had been fucking some-*
*one when he was out of town on business.*

### Katie, college student, Missouri (913-205-XXXX)

My brother and I had to listen to my mom fucking all the men she brought home in the next room....I did all the cooking and cleaning and took care of my brother. Sometimes there wasn't any food.... Dad abandoned us and Mom's brilliant—a criminal, immoral, selfish whore, an abusive bitch, amongst other things....At my high school graduation my mom told me she was taking my brother away and I'd never see him again....I want to work for the UN.

### Holly, 26, Wisconsin

Dad beat me, my sister, and my mom, and he finally got arrested. He went to prison and a mental institution....I went through a bunch of foster homes....He tried to contact me on Facebook, but I didn't respond....I tried to kill myself at 17 with an overdose of sleeping pills. The ambulance took me away.

### 678-314-XXXX

I got a car and a job and I moved out of the house at 16....Just the way things needed to happen.

*When Kira was 15, she stopped going to class. Her par-*
*ents sent her to San Diego to live with her grandparents.*
*They thought a change of scenery might help. I can just*
*imagine quirky, lanky Kira—she was 5'11" when she was*
*15—hanging out with her hard-drinking Sicilian grandma.*
*I'm obsessed with that, actually. I can see Kira taking every-*

*thing in and asking her manic grandma a million questions. I can see them burning around San Diego in that convertible Mustang, shooting whiskey. I'd love to somehow go back in time and watch those two.*

## Gabrielle

Hello, Jeff. I need some moral guidance, and I was hoping you could help. I've been living with my grandma all my life. Mom and Dad left me behind. And I never see them. I've tried to kill myself 5 times in 2 years. My grandma hates me because I'm bi. I'm currently a thief and I steal to survive. I need to know how I can make it without stealing or lying.

*Kira's younger sister, who was always pointing her finger at me, stole $10,000 from her mom along with her car and took off to the Midwest when she was 16. She came back with a baby.*

## Marine, San Diego (715-410-XXXX)

Honestly, man, if it wasn't for the Marines I'd probably be a lowlife because of my past and family before I was 18.

## Brittany

My mother's 2nd pregnancy ended at 4 months after she had a heart attack at age 21. The baby died inside her. After the baby died, Dad was angry all the time and he abused her. After she finally moved out, taking shelter with the father of a family friend, she received death threats from my dad. He was a military man and used to perfection.

*I want to have a family and love my family and have a house filled with animals: dogs, cats, rabbits, fish. All I want out of life is to love my family and animals. I want to walk with my wife and kids and dogs every night, hugging and holding them, laughing, playing. I want to have a garden. I want to roll in the dirt with my kids. Play hide-and-seek. Have my dogs sniffing every plant and bush in the garden. I want to teach my kids to love animals and nature. I thought I could have all this with Kira.*

**305-773-XXXX**

It's a struggle between my parents and my heart.

*My dad didn't call 911 when he was having his second heart attack. Instead, he got dressed and drove to my house, which was a few miles away. He knocked on my door. I was out to dinner. He got back in his truck, drove a block, got out, and died in front of my neighbor's house with a nitroglycerin pill under his tongue. I drove up on my dad's body.*

**Brittany**

She went from being my mom to being my child. We were bowling at the alley on our military base. Mom took one step toward the foul line and cracked her femur all the way down the center like a giant, ugly fissure. Seven years and 3 failed surgeries later, she still can't walk. Sometimes I blame myself. Since her injury, my mother has had to be on many strong and varied medicines. I'm of the suspicion that they, along with the pain and the mental trauma of not being able to walk, are what changed her. It's like her past decided to catch up. Her dad used to beat her until she ran away from home. She went from loving me to depending on me. Simply put, my mom died, and in her place I was given the responsibility of taking care of a psychotic, hateful child.

### Girl, 18, Denver (303-217-XXXX)
I was in a fight with my mother yesterday....She wouldn't stop acting like a child and I exploded on her and started crying, left the house. I hate it....Thank you...She's stubborn. And she won't respect me....I was going to call you, but I didn't know if you were busy or not.

### Dana, 21, college student and babysitter
My mom died in Mexico during childbirth when I was 8. She tried to save money by going to a cheap doctor in Mexico City. The doctor didn't do a sonogram and took the baby out wrong. Mom lost too much blood and she and the baby died.

*Kira was pregnant. We were going to be a family. She has never forgotten the ghost image of the ultrasound heartbeat. She lost the baby. She was never well after that, so sad and mourning.*

### Caitlin
My sister has a degenerative brain disease. The doctors really don't know much about it or what to do.

### Susie (469-335-XXXX)
I'm a security officer married to an abusive man. I've been very worried about my 2-year-old because she started hitting her head on

things and purposely running into walls. I googled it and found out that when children can't verbalize things, they hit themselves. I'm very relieved.

## Lauren, 19, New Mexico

When I was living in Oakland with my dad, I smashed some kid's head into a locker and got kicked out of high school.... Year probation and 40 hours community service—I think they overreacted....I loved Vegas, but my mom got transferred and Albuquerque sucks....I don't know anybody now and sit around at home a lot.

*I told Lauren to get out and meet people any way she can.*

## Amy

I'm driving by the sex party house tonight to see if it looks alright, if it looks safe. If it doesn't, there's no way I go. Babysitters are expensive. You want to come with?

## Jasmine (209-202-XXXX)

Should I give my boyfriend a bj right now?....I'm 23 and a mom.... I was horny then. I used my porn and squirt and other toys—now I'm good.

*It's over. I'll never be able to love animals with Kira again or watch how amazing she is with children. I can't accept it. Today I came to the realization that I have to quit art and just help people.*

## Samantha, 22, Portland Community College student (503-247-XXXX)

I still like to party sometimes and dance all night in clubs....We lived on a farm outside Portland and I was really happy. When I was 10, my parents got heavily into cocaine and wrecked everything. We lost the farm. Mom and Dad got arrested for possession. We had to go to family counseling. That's when I first heard from them the stories of the wild parties and crazy orgies. I missed a large part of childhood because of their coke habit. I partied hard for a couple of years after I turned 15....I was flunking out of school and lost the part-time jobs I had. I was promiscuous too....I mean I still love sex—who doesn't?... It scares me that both of my parents are addicts. I could easily slip into their lifestyle....I'm a freshman and I want to be a physician.

*Samantha loves to take care of her body. She sent me photos. She's 5'7", 115 pounds, delicate features, auburn hair, wondrous brown eyes. Extremely attractive. Star quality.*

## Ashley

I did some community theatre in my teens. My mother made me, since I was home-schooled and so introverted. I loathed it the first year but grew to love it. It taught me how to bullshit. I think it had to do with wearing different masks and finding out that confidence is 90 percent of it. If need be, I can command anyone's attention just by faking that charisma and forwardness.

*Every year my parents would go to Hawaii for three weeks. When Mom would pick us up, she'd always overact in front of my babysitter, hanging on every word my brother and I said. When we'd get in the car, the detachment would start.*

## 336-267-XXXX

Do you like Peter Gabriel's "Big Time"? Are you larger than life? You bout to be raided bitch.

*In rages I can even understand WWII tyrants. It comes from a lack of love throughout my life, isolation, and pain. I can't believe how asinine people are when they ask, "How can someone like Hitler exist?" I can be riding the subway, wanting to blow up the entire world, then five minutes later I can look at a young child and start crying.*

## Karen

How can we get uninterested kids interested in subjects they don't like?

*I told Karen to tell them parables and fables to get them excited about the subject matter.*

## 509-703-XXXX

*A 17-year-old girl from Spokane dreams of being a film director. Either comedies or thrillers. Her mother abandoned her at birth. Her father and stepmother are abusive. She's living with her 16-year-old brother. No guardians, just those two. Her brother cooks because she doesn't know how to. She's extremely nice. She texted me, "I need to tell you I get crushes on any guys who are nice to me. I don't want to get hurt." She's texting me constantly. "Would you date an*

*18-year-old?" I need to tell her that we can only be friends. I don't want to hurt her. I want to help her.*

## Cleo (917-509-XXXX)

There's a whole world out there, and me and my high school girl-friends are in here talking about our petty problems. I like what you're doing.

*At 5:05, on 7-22-11, I was on a United Airlines 747 taxiing down the JFK runway. I was heading to LA for Tim Caviezel's 40th birthday. (Tim is the actor Jim Caviezel's brother. We all grew up together north of Seattle.) Window seat. There was a Pakistani woman next to me, kind of chunky, and in the aisle seat was an adorable girl. I wanted to play with the pretty girl and her siblings, but how do you do that without looking like a pedo? I love making faces at children. It's fun trying to make them laugh. "Mom, would I die if I fell out of the airplane while it's still on the runway?" I love these kids' curiosity. "Mom, why's there smoke coming from above the window?" "That's not smoke, honey. It's steam." The girl was munching on a huge chocolate chip cookie. She was taking her finger and rubbing it on the chocolate, then putting her finger on her tongue. I hope that tongue never gets pierced.*

## Kimberly (347-451-XXXX)

I'm ur lil pinches

*I should have never rescued Kira. I'm not the rescuing type.*

## 715-771-XXXX

I like it rough, doggy style, and being on the bottom....I want to fuck you too. Would you fuck me till it hurt?... Merci....But when I'm a good little girl, will you make the pain go away?... Baby, I'm your little whore. Will you punish me when I'm a bad girl?... Promise me that, baby....If I cried, you'd just cradle me, right?

*I'm falling in love with so many of these women. It's hypnotic. I want to take care of all of them and their families.*

## 478-213-XXXX

You're on my phone under "Batman" and I don't understand why. Do you enjoy being "Batman"?

## Denise

Pay me child support. 'Cause these kids ain't gonna pay themselves. Better call me back, chico. Remember? The Bronx?

## Krystal

I have sex with men for cash. Im a bad person....The others do it too....I will get in trouble if I call now. I can text....How am I not? I do horrible things....I got out....Mark said he had a lot to offer....If I can get out, would you take me?... After I graduate?... That's not until June. I don't want to do this for another year....I left my brother with the rents....He can't help me. Mark takes care of me now....He allows me to have a roof over my head and buys me clothes....If you can't because I'm 17, take me in then....I guess it would....I don't want to listen to men anymore but if I don't I get in trouble....I'd rather be living with you....I want to be normal....I dont want to be hurt....He takes advantage of me in front of others....Im scared....I do feel horrible though....I feel gross and used. I feel like no man can ever love me...Mainly for what I have to do....One time I actually had an orgasm while making money. I felt so disgusting....I didn't do it to feel good. It just happened....I wasn't in control, the way he had me positioned and pinned....I don't know. There was something inside of me....I'm sorry....I don't want to get you into trouble....Still be friends?... I get a free breakfast and lunch at school so I do eat....We almost died, Jeff, but it was fun!... Black ice on highway, 2 wheel drive...We swerved into the other lane and drifted and did a Uturn. Other cars honked and had to slow....I do, but I wasn't driving. I dont have my license....I have no choice. I have to go to school....Hey talk to me....I'm bored....Hes my boss....I am not a hooker....Ok I believe you....I know that's what it is, but I don't get to keep most of the $—it goes to Matt....What do you consider it?... I have to do it though....I don't have control of it. He pays for it....I want out. But I can't. I don't have anywhere else to go and I wouldn't be able to support myself....My stepmom wont deal with me....I want to be 18 so bad. What if I had a fake ID? Could I come live with you then?... Ill be in this situation for the rest of my life....Steal me....I want to leave....He could hurt me....Jeff?... Thank you....That's so cool! I would love to write. I have a book written but its not published of course....I don't need help. Don't get me help....Just let it be....Forget it. Just be my friend. That's all I need....Just be my friend. That's it....Please don't try to get anyone involved. I'm fine....Thanks. I will go away this weekend....I bet it's so loud where you are....Where do you think I should go?... Hey talk to me.

*I'd go in their room and they'd always be passed out; Mom would be spread-eagle. Dad would get up and walk nude to the bathroom. After Mom died, Dad's new wife, Patti, would get drunk and make fun of the fact that Mom used a dildo. The babysitter always asked me what was wrong.*

# III. Love Sucks

**Gretchen**

You have your phone forwarding and you're lonely? I was going to give you pussy.

**224-622-XXXX**

I have the weirdest boner right now.

**903-931-XXXX**

Can I get a picture first? No offense, but I've been lied to before....I need to know who I'm talking to because if that's you in those pictures, then I'm good.

**616-821-XXXX**

Woot score 1 for the cool chicka...Oh dear lord or dear lordy-lordysweetums...I'm 17 dear lordy and this is massively inappropriate Jeffrey!... Lol! We mustn't continue this....Ohh, why can't we be friends?... I guess...No creeper stuff, you old fart!... Mr. Lonely Jeff are you drunk?... You sure seem to like complimenting people.... You're chipper dude....I hope you find an equal chipper sweetie.

## Brianna (509-281-XXXX)

It was delightful except for this delusional old bastard hitting on me all night.

## Andrea (636-209-XXXX)

*Andrea sends a picture of herself on a boat on the Hudson, squeezing an exposed breast and sticking her tongue out.*

I want to punch Kira in the pussy for breaking up with you. I'm gonna punch your ex in the puss! Kira is getting fucked right now!

## Betsy (636-209-XXXX)

I wish I was on a train with you....I would want you to finger me, get me wet, then find a side street and fuck me from behind. Hard!

## Ashley

I would indeed like a rather large penis at the moment.

## Jenna

If she left, she'll be back.

## Courtney, 21, college student, North Carolina State University

My boyfriend and I split up over the summer, cuz he was with other women....My friends told me to leave him: "be strong." Now he wants me back and calls me daily, saying he loves me....I don't know what to do. My friends are biased....I'm torn. I'll always think about the fact that he slept with other women, people I know. It won't leave my head. What should I do?

## Billie

You can do anything you set your mind to!... I want to see you.... I think just you and I can do that—not everyone....We could do wonderful amazing things....We just have to make sure the physical chemistry is there!... So you tell me a plan!

## Cassandra (501-208-XXXX)

Thanks for the pic....I love the head of your cock....I'm transfixed by the beauty of your member actually....So well rounded at the tip... Such a pronounced groove at the head's base for ribbed stimulation....You are very close in size to my current beau....I le disappeared....Sigh...By which I mean he promised to keep in touch but has been MIA the last 10 days.

## Valerie (973-283-XXXX)

My boyfriend and I broke up, but now we're like friends with benefits. We still have sex and say I love you and all that, except I say it more often to him.

## Helen, 23, Stockton, California

I just got a new tattoo and have been thinking about what I wanna do with my life....As of now I'm just having fun with my guy. Who knows what will happen?... I try to believe in soul mates, but it's hard to keep the optimism alive. I used to think my ex and I were soul mates; sometimes I still do, because we always wind up in each other's lives, but people come and go and I just try to enjoy them while they're there.

## Heather

I don't like dating. You can't trust new people....I am in a relationship, though....It's the first time I've ever been with a guy who treats me really nice. In the Bronx, all my boyfriends were gangster types....All my friends know him, so I can't ask other guys for their numbers in front of everybody....He's really nice, but I feel stuck with nice.

## Bethany, 24, White Plains, NY (845-282-XXXX)

I like a guy who is sweet but an asshole at the same time. He can't be overly sweet—that's just a pussy.

## Ashley

I'm glad you agree on the nice part....We were both rather intoxicated. It wasn't anything too complex. Just a nice 15-minute lay.... Naw, he didn't finish....It felt great, although we were in the dark....I miss you too, weirdly.

## Lindsey, 23, Wisconsin (920-475-XXXX)

This relationship thing is at 6 months and first he didn't tell me bout 3 DUIs....Probably he's alcoholic and anyway he's gonna do jail soon for last one....He's pleading house arrest....Is it gonna take me down? He's a one man wrecking crew....Getting the fuck away from him is confusing.

## Ashley

We were both too drunk to come, though....The best was a navy sergeant. He was covered in tattoos and the whole thing felt so taboo....When I was 18, I was raped by an army serviceman....I think it was the whole idea of hooking up with another military man. Both terrifying and titillating. Perhaps that was the subconscious motive behind some of my past promiscuity? Reclaiming my sense of control over sex.

**Erica**

Jeff, why were you so doubtful of me coming at first?

**Ashley**

I hardly ever make noise when I come. I just shiver and shake.

**Man from Ontario**

I had sex for the first time when I was 18. I said, "I love you," and she didn't say it back. It jaded me.

**Ashley**

I think I could love you. I feel like that's difficult to say never having even touched you....But I love the idea of you....That's very true about women my age....Old man :)...I think I'm very fluid.

**Carla, American short story writer living in the Netherlands**

Bad relationships have always fueled creativity. I'm glad I've been neglected. I'd be at IBM if I hadn't.

**Hannah, writer, 27 (215-554-XXXX)**

Nice! I'm writing a semi-autobiographical novel about being a second-generation punk fuck living in Philadelphia squalor in a quasi-lesbian relationship.

**Jasmyn, short story writer (631-559-XXXX)**

I'll call you later if I get drunk and want to talk about sex.

**Eduardo (908-937-XXXX)**

She was the dumbest girl I ever knew, but her body was worth it.

**336-267-XXXX**

Dude, you're fucking hot. Do you have a big dick?

**Ashley**

To be completely honest, the biggest guy I've ever been with was a longtime friend who was a skinny computer geek, 22, and a virgin. I told him I wanted to finally introduce him to the wonders of sex. And he would not believe me when I told him how unusually large he was. I bled the whole time....No, I didn't come. It was like having a Mercedes and a learner's permit. I hope someday he learns to drive....He was a doll, though.

**Cheryl**

Are you cut or uncut? I love men cut. So much more friction.

**16-year-old high school wrestler**

I took her to the movie last Friday and was the perfect gentleman, paid for the movie, opened doors. Kissed her in the theater. She doesn't want to be with me anymore....I know, that's like what I thought at first. I was too nice—girls need a challenge, a guy who doesn't treat them so nice, but I don't know....I found out she didn't like my kisses. Fuck...Yeah, but my last girlfriend was a slut, seeing a bunch of guys all at once. She gave my best friend a hand job and blow job.

## Rita

Hooked up with a guy. He won't call. I feel used....Yeah, I wanted it too.

## 860-739-XXXX

I don't trust women. Sometimes you find a woman who's genuinely amazing. I know those are the ones that you never want to get over.

## Darryl, bartender, 27, NYC (646-249-XXXX)

He started to get really possessive and jealous. Then he stopped having sex and broke up with her. Took her 6 months to get over it. She's happy she went through it, though it was horrible. She lost 20 pounds, couldn't eat. Went out drinking a lot. She grew and learned about herself.

## Valerie (973-283-XXXX)

I work out a lot at the gym and don't eat exactly, sometimes not at all....My boyfriend would come over and leave immediately if I hadn't worked out yet because I would be bonkers....He got really upset when I wouldn't eat because he said I had no energy....The breakup was crazy bad intense.

## Tito, 37, NYC

For months after, I couldn't sleep or eat. Didn't think I could go on.

*I met Tito on the street while taping up a flyer; he'd just gone through an awful breakup.*

## Florida man (305-799-XXXX)

Been stood up bad....Hate 'em.

**973-518-XXXX**

I went out with this guy for 8 months. He came over for the last time, looked around, then left....Guys are really weird sometimes.... I smoke a lot of weed and just chill.

**Jack**

I don't fall in love. I love jazz.

**Ashley**

I haven't fucked in nearly a year....I'd love to break my dry spell with you....I'm not doing anyone from here. I have a No Fuck Policy for this county...Which has made me very frustrated the last 4 months.

**Shannon, 24, prostitute/stripper/porn star, living in Vancouver, BC**

> *Currently works in a brothel. Intelligent. Reading Poe and Anne Rice. Her family has no idea what she does. She says her family is redneck stock, so she tells them she works in a gay bar, knowing they won't enter a gay bar. She's traveling right now for a month in Australia and New Zealand. She's incredibly hot. Many sexy pictures on her Facebook page. In Vancouver, where she escorts, prostitution's legal. In the U.S., it's illegal. She says we're a Puritan country, repressed and backward. Which—no duh. We've talked for many hours on the phone. She has an escort ad that shows photos of her scantily clad. At the bottom of her ad runs a caption: "The best thing since Jesus." She wants me to visit her in Canada when she gets back from her vacation. She's written me twice from New Zealand, saying*

*she misses our phone calls. She also wants me to go on a U.S. escort tour with her. I'd accompany her all over the U.S. and live in hotels while she escorts and makes tons of money. I told her I would love to do this.*

### 516-582-XXXX

*(I say I'm going to Vegas and ask her if she wants to go with me— my treat.)....*Maybe. You cute?... *(I send her a pic.)....*Not bad, but I'm better looking. Here's a picture of me and my friends in a club. I'm a party girl. High maintenance!...*(I ask her what she's doing tomorrow.)....*I'm partying in Manhattan....*(This is actually a good reality show premise—how many people would go on vacations with people they don't know?)*

### Ashley

Well, here we go again. Drunk and horny...You are an excellent drunken sexting buddy you know that....I don't know how it is for men. But for me, everything feels hot and swollen and sensitive and desperate for touch.

### Jessie, 14-year-old from Queens, NY

Tranny Alert...masturbating on subway platform

### Nursing student, 22, Texas (210-838-XXXX)

I like my friend's neighbor. I've only seen him once. How should I approach him?

### JD (914-215-XXXX)

Should I be aggressive or let her come to me?

## Walgreens employee, 24, Michigan (248-343-XXXX)

Sup Jeff...I'm just at work at Walgreens. Pretty slow night...I'm actually trying to date the girl who works in the pharmacy here but it's not going so well....Well she's currently dating the manager here but she gives me a glance every now and then that makes me think I might have a chance....Thanks for your support. You're probably right. Shaky territory.

## Erica

I would love for someone to touch my body who wouldn't be disgusted by me....You would be disgusted by my fat—even I am.... You're just being nice....I had a threesome....Anyways, hi.

## Kenny

Hi, Jeff. My boyfriend and I were sitting here looking through pictures online and we came across your number and I can't believe that this is for real. But if you're that lonely, here's 2 pix of goodhearted guys and a dog that would love to talk to you. I don't know why, but we would. Guess we're a little lonely too. Call us. Bye.

## Samantha

*She was doing her nails while talking to me. She's been in a relationship for a couple months. When she met the guy, she wasn't into him. He called a few times and she didn't respond. He ended up taking her and a couple of her friends to dinner and a Mariners game. Samantha liked that he was old-fashioned: he brought her flowers when he picked her up. Persistency paid off. Samantha said she wasn't interested in him at all, but after all the calls and the Mariners*

*game, she caved in. I've always heard this from women. The*
*guy who keeps calling them ends up with them.*

## Meredith (646-943-XXXX)

I was thinking about that first night we were texting, how you said that all you ever wanted was love...& I thought maybe I could love you...umm

## Erica

I'm not perfect, Jeff. You deserve so much better than me.

## 617-921-XXXX

Anyone currently stealing your heart?

## Brittany

Yes, I cum very easily :-)....Yes, I loved the 9 inch cock. It felt great....Well, the smaller ones I've been with were thicker so they felt just as good....There are several suitors now....They've all volunteered, but only one that I've let...The last time we were together was a little over a week ago and I came 4 times in the car....He really wants to fuck me in the ass,,,,I'll keep you posted

## 321-402-XXXX

Did you ever try going out, Jeff? Clubs? Bars? The library? The park? The supermarket? Gas station? I'm out of places.

## Vanessa, 22, Minnesota

My best friend was naked, hiding in the bathroom. He was still lying in bed when I walked in on them. I dated him for 2 years, thought

I was going to marry him....I'm a psych major. I like rock climbing, snowmobiling, and skeet shooting....I didn't kill him because I was too devastated. A year later I met Jared. He's the love of my life.

### Olivia, 22 (347-453-XXXX)

My boyfriend never takes my advice on anything....He thinks I'm stupid pretty much and I guess he's right about that too. He never wants to comfort me when I'm sad because he doesn't like it when I'm sad, which I guess is normal....I spent all of yesterday sleeping and vomiting....I don't want to go back to rehab. It would mean I failed at my attempt at recovery. I never want to go back there....It wasn't a horrible place or anything. Everyone was extremely sweet and kind and it was a nice living environment, but I would just never want to go back. Plus I need to get on with my life....I just need to figure out how. I've been taking a long time trying to figure out how, though....I know you probably think, "Oh, she can't possibly have an eating disorder because she's not nearly too thin," but it is possible because I suffer from bulimia, not anorexia....Yesterday I told my boyfriend I felt like a loser, and he didn't disagree with me. He said he was a loser also and then went on to talk about his problem trying to find a good personal trainer....I want to get in touch with old friends but I doubt they really care—do you think they'd care? Maybe not? Hmm...Sorry if I'm bombarding you with all this crap, but I don't have therapy till tomorrow and you're a great listener. Oh, well...I guess you don't care, either. What happened? You used to respond quickly and like me a lot more....For future reference, please tell me everything I said/did wrong.

### Clark (212-470-XXXX)

So are you married?

# IV. Love Really Sucks

**956-648-XXXX**

Ruined…Think my ex is already talking to someone else and we've been only broken up for a month and were together almost 3 years….Time doesn't do anything….It brings in more pain.

*This woman has called twice with a restricted number. She works in Manhattan in the financial sector. The second time she called, she was crying. She and her boyfriend broke up a year and a half ago. He graduated from West Point and got deployed, and she couldn't take the long-distance relationship. He told her recently that he loves his new girlfriend. She told me she's been dating but that her new boyfriend, though nice and good-looking, isn't like her true love. She's worried that her ex is the love of her life and that he got away. Even when she looks at her new boyfriend, her ex comes into her head. She knows this isn't fair to her current boyfriend. She's really convinced she'll never love anyone like her ex. Her voice was cracking as she was saying this. She says she thinks about him every day. That the weirdest things come to her. She'll be filing something, and her ex will pop into her head. Something they did—a walk,*

*a movie they enjoyed together. I told her I was sorry, that I*
*completely understand.*

### Brooke, 36, Upper West Side (917-376-XXXX)

My dad died when I was young. Mom took copious medications after he died and checked out emotionally....I was 17 when I met this Andy Warholesque artist who was a genius, but he could never put it all together. We'd get major commercial offers for his work, set up a meeting, and he would walk out of the meeting, killing the whole deal. He never achieved the financial success he could have....We were together 17 years. When we broke up, we couldn't figure out why we were still together; it didn't seem like there was a point to the relationship anymore. And that was after couples therapy for years. If both people aren't working at it, the therapy—it's useless....My sister and brother do the same thing: long relationships, usually around 10 years, then they end the relationships. Maybe a pattern set by Dad's death. We seem to lack the tools to go the long run....I get lonely. New York is a hard place to meet people. If you do, they just want to jump in the sack the first date....I make great money as an investment banker, but some things I just can't figure out, and I don't think I ever will, love being one of them.

### Woman, 25, NYC (347-878-XXXX)

I was seeing my roommate's friend and I really liked him. Wonderful chemistry. I thought it was one of those rare connections between 2 people. He stopped calling. When I see him, he pretends like nothing ever happened....I want closure, don't know how to get over it.

**Jenna, Memphis (901-568-XXXX)**

Yeah, I totally lost it...Assaulted him. I even went to jail....Not my proudest moment. I honestly believe anyone else would have done it....I always wanted to have 1 more child since I was so young with my only daughter....We were going through the adoption process....Two months before we were ready to get our child my husband cancelled it....Being a mom was/is everything to me.... The charge was expunged after a year for being good....Things have never been the same at home....I feel like he's just not into me.

**Ariel (770-842-XXXX)**

Gotta go. My husband just found these texts. It was nice talking to you. I doubt it'll happen again.

*When Kira told me she loved someone else, I lost it. I got drunk and wrote her emails telling her off. The police called me and said they wanted to talk to Kira and me. I thought it was a ploy to get me to come to the station to arrest me, so I didn't go. I told Detective Alvarez that I'd be out of town until November 1 and then I'd come in. Apparently Kira told him this wasn't true. A week later Alvarez called me and said he was at my apartment building and that my apartment number didn't exist. (I had originally given him the wrong address on purpose.) I told him I was still out of town and that he should contact my lawyer from now on. He was there to arrest me. An hour later he called back and said to tell my lawyer there was now a warrant for my arrest. He ended with "Have a nice day." A couple days later Kira emailed me, saying the only reason Alvarez put a warrant out was because I wouldn't talk to him. She said the legal issue was now between Alvarez and me. So I am a famous internet personality ("Lonely Jeff") and a wanted man. I still don't know what I'm charged with.*

## Krystal

If I lived with you in real life would you hit me?... Do you think I'm pretty?... I don't want to fight with you, but I do like your dominance over me....Why don't you want to be with me?... I can't talk. I'm in the car with my parents ... I know, I'm only 17....Kidnap me.... Please Jeff....How old are you again?... You're basically the same age as my dad, that's why I can't tell them....If I lived with you I would want to take showers with you....I love you Jeff. You care about me....I will be with you someday Jeff, I know it....As long as you don't start drama or I'll blackmail you....I like you a lot but want to be able to trust you.

## Jenna

U can stalk me if u want....Give me something worthy to write about.

## 29-year-old woman, New Jersey

Crying. I hate it and do it too much.

## 917-325-XXXX

Relationships are best with no-contact orders.

## Molly

I hate it when you say you'll try to see me :(

*The word* divorce *was scarier than AIDS. I'd get over-whelmed thinking about having someone new in the house. Mom threatened Dad with divorce daily.*

**A man in Mexico**
My girlfriend left me. I almost fucking killed her.

**Ashley**
I'd love to spoon you and have you choke me gently from behind....I just had the best orgasm thinking of you....I love a light choking.

**217-691-XXXX**
Hey bitchfacecuntbucket.

**Erica**
Jack cheated on me constantly. And he has anger issues. I'm afraid he might hurt me or hate me.

*My life's all-time low was when I had sex with a 75-pound Asian hooker I knew had AIDS, but I was so screwed up on coke and alcohol I didn't even care. I actually felt sorry for her because she had to pay for the cab ride over to the hotel I was staying in. She got on top of me, and it was like screwing a skeleton. I couldn't even look at her.*

**Jenna**
I guess because I've been hurt so bad, nothing else can hurt me.... Yeah, porn is not realistic to me unless the chick has dirty feet and a pimple on at least one butt cheek....I'm married, so yeah I watch

porn more than I'm willing to admit....If I were you I'd skip the whole married thing and just have kids....The idea of marriage is great, but getting 2 people to share the same goals is unrealistic.

### 19-year-old guy, Brooklyn

"Don't chase 'em, Replace 'em" Notorious BIG.

### Ashley

The summer of '10, I was intoxicated by the thrill of hooking up and reeling in a man for casual sex. I had 5 men in 2 months.

### 586-337-XXXX

Quick question: have you ever raped, murdered, or kidnapped anyone?

### Ashley

I just had sex again....Ironically I was trying to recreate u, his name is Jeff 2.... We did spooning then doggy....Very thick but not really long....I miss you 2....I try. It's hard when ur always getting lambasted.

### Murph, Brooklyn (904-517-XXXX)

We're smokin' trees, man....We got a couple girls at our lair and we're lookin' to gangbang. Oh yeeeeah!

### Richard

Do you have any fantasies that you didn't get to explore in your relationship with Kira?... There's life after a breakup....That's a tough one....Are you into cross-dressing?

**Karl (718-709-XXXX)**

Not too well, just had a huge breakup and my girlfriend isn't taking me back.

**Marianne**

My bf and I are angry and fighting all the time. I don't want to let stupid stuff get in the way anymore.

*I'd never dealt with being hit like that. Kira and I had just been in a fight. She was going through Klonopin withdrawals and punching me repeatedly. It made me crazy.*

**682-999-XXXX**

I stopped taking birth control because the pills make me feel crazy. I feel like my boyfriend is ignoring me. He cares about hockey more than he does me. I need him right now. I didn't want to go to his hockey game and he wouldn't sit out 1 game for me.

**616-821-XXXX**

I loved him to death, but he was a real drill hole and wasn't going anywhere and was dragging me down with him and the breakup was something that had to happen for me to realize that, so I guess behind every dark cloud is a ray of sunshine poking its head out.

**646-553-XXXX**

Yo, meet me at Bronx River Projects, Made Bitch...... PS: Bring a gun.

*With Leslie it was the last thing I could do to get back at her. I got drunk and sent her an email saying I was going to kill her and that I knew this was a felony threat, but I didn't care because if I went to jail, it would just motivate me more to kill her when I got out. She didn't email me back. And she didn't have my current phone number. A year later I was blacked out at my brother's in Bellingham, and I called Leslie's phone and left my brother's number. The next morning the Berkeley police called. My brother answered and said he'd have me call them back. I called and spoke to an officer. I lied and said I hadn't sent a death threat. I told him someone must have hacked my email account.*

### Valerie (973-283-XXXX)

I saw your youtube. You are a bundle of energy which is cool because I can be too. You seem like someone who could keep up with me. Are you a good man?

### Woman, 47, Florida

*Her husband was in prison for five years (insurance fraud: he burnt his office building down and tried to collect). She was devoted to him his entire stay. She found out, after he was released, that he had girls coming to see him during visits. He immediately divorced her when he got out and went off with another woman (younger, too). She feels completely used: "I'll never get those five years back."*

### Valerie (973-283-XXXX)

Last weekend I told my boyfriend I was feeling guilty after eating.... He told me to go throw up....Right now, not great. Kinda feeling terrible...My boyfriend's pretty much the only person I have to talk about it with and to be honest he doesn't really seem to care.... Also, I think my therapist is an idiot....My therapist told me I should consider becoming a housewife, wtf?... I'd really rather just be friends with him....He's a great friend but he doesn't know how to be supportive....I think it'd be better for me to be with someone who eats normally and is not concerned with weight issues....We never go out to restaurants which makes me feel kind of sad...Because we did when we first started going out and it was so romantic.... He also used to buy me all the drinks I wanted....But then he limited it to 1 and now he won't even buy me 1 drink....I'm not allowed to drink anymore anyway....Well I'm allowed to but I really shouldn't because the last time I drank I was a total mess....I drank on an empty stomach and mixed pot which was a very bad idea....I had to force myself to throw up just to get some of the alcohol out of my system and I passed out on the street....My boyfriend had sex with me that night....He said I was too drunk but I was like let's do it anyway....At least that's what he said....But then I felt bad in the morning....I thought maybe he should have realized that I was too drunk to make that decision....And then he said from that point on 1 drink....And if I pass out on the street he's going to leave me there.

**762-901-XXXX**

I keep changing my number....My sister's abusive husband I think is pranking.

**Tara (770-276-XXXX)**

I thought you were Jeff. I'm sorry...Oh...I'm good. So what do you want to talk about?... Sorry about your breakup....I don't know how to help you there.

## 347-451-XXXX

I just really wanted u....We should probably stop talking....I just developed feelings 4 u....Don't want that happening....I'm really young and need to go for someone my own age....Glad you understand. It does but im only 18....No don't say that baby....Move on ok?... Find a beautiful sweet girl....You deserve the best!... It was nice talking to u....So goodbye forever, Jeff.

## Leah, 27

I met a guy in the Hamptons on Memorial Day. We've been together for 5 months....He recently lost his dad and had just come out of a long-term relationship. I don't know if he's stable enough to make a decision....Should I move on? We have a good time together, but I just don't know if he's in the right state of mind from all the trauma.

## Kimberly

I'm too picky and needy for you....I want to wake up to you everyday....Not the right person for you...Just plz find someone else, or in this case let someone find u lol....U know the whole phn thing... Lots of luvly girls 4 u :)....Sorry for being a bitch. I rlly like u n wanna be with u.

> *Kira was fully aware that telling me she loved someone else would set me off. She knows, however, I would never hurt her. Even after we broke up she called, crying and saying she loved me.*

**Parker (family fight in background)**

Hi, it's Parker. How are you? *(Screaming in background: "Fuck off!")* I wanted to talk because I'm lonely too. *(Man grabs phone from Parker: "Don't ever talk to my daughter again! Understand me?")*

**404-917-XXXX**

Love? You hardly even know me....It's dangerous to love me....I hurt people that love me.

**Erica**

I'm so sorry we destroyed ourselves....Your soul has lost its worth to me.

# V. Problems

*All the money I won on Whoopi Goldberg's game show,* Head Games, *has evaporated.*

### Widow, 60, Westchester, New York (914-576-XXXX)

New York died before 9/11. It's just about greed now, full of arrogant shitheads....One daughter, she's 29, has a master's in communications. She works as a nanny. The other is unemployed, living with her boyfriend.

### Goldman Sachs trader (212-357-XXXX)

I'm not doing that well....I'm calling strangers who post flyers on the internet from my trading desk....The economy's in a major downturn and we have Occupy Wall Street keeping us prisoner. It's combative. We're under siege down here.

### Middle Eastern man, 27, NYC

*Lives with parents. Did three years of college. Can't seem to find work. Dreams of being an architect but must go back to school and finish his degree. He thinks New Yorkers are hard to meet. He wouldn't tell me what country he was from in the Middle East. I sensed he felt I'd judge him in post-9/11 America.*

**Olivia**

A lil optimistic. Hopefully will stay that way fingers crossed want to spend the day looking for a job....Yesterday was a mess. Lotsa mixed feelings, doubts, nausea.

**Patience, 23, NYC**

My friends have deserted me since I got pregnant. They still go out at night and hit the clubs....It's hard for me to want to go out. I mostly stay inside and eat....I work in a doctor's office as a secretary....He gives me some money....No, we're not together.

*I suggested Patience get the father's payments as a legally binding doc.*

**Sorority sisters**

Are you rich?

**John (978-476-XXXX)**

I'm sort of a recluse. I like having people to interact with, but it stresses me out for some reason. It's hard to explain. Sometimes I wonder if there's something wrong with me.

**Mark, 28, NYC**

I'm a choreographer and everyone in the arts is out of work. I've been very depressed. I can't pay my bills.

**423-946-XXXX**

Even fast food places aren't hiring.

### Aaron, Memphis (901-341-XXXX)

Memphis is dangerous, violent, in disarray, riled with gang activity. My wife wants to move. I'd just as well stay.

### College girl, Silicon Valley

I went through a traumatic breakup. Now I want to work in finance.

### Kristina (301-339-XXXX)

I work in politics....I want to marry a Jewish guy but there aren't that many in DC.

> *Kristina and her friend texted me a photo-booth photo of them with the text message "Breakups are lame."*

### 19-year-old girl, Texas

I need your opinion, Jeff. My first love has been deployed overseas but is coming home. I've been living with this other guy for 2 years. Who should I go with? I'm leaning toward the military man because he has a good job, pension, security.

### Jenna

There is a Jeff Ragsdale who sings the national anthem on YouTube. I think he's totally trying to steal street cred from you.

### Tucker

My uncle was going to afghanistan and on his way to his final briefing, a couple hours before he was supposed to board the plane in dc, he got hit by a dump truck and died....His wife wanted him to quit the military cuz of the dangers....My dad's a drunk.

**Jerry**

I just went through a divorce and then lost my job. I'm under terrible crushing debt.

**Second marine in California (218-640-XXXX)**

Back from Honduras deployment where I got ejected out of a Humvee, crash landed 38 feet away against a stop sign...Broken hand, wrist, nine ribs, cut up all to shit...I'm on disability leave.

**860-682-XXXX**

My life is fucked up. I'm a graffiti artist and people keep destroying my work and the cops keep arresting me.

**Tyrone, 27, NYC (917-701-XXXX)**

I came up here from South Carolina for work about 5 years ago, lost the job, and now I'm stressed....No, no family here...I'm not a people person—even job interviews are tough....I'd go to counseling but don't have the cash....At times I don't know who I am. It's like I get lost inside my selves.

**Egyptian student, 17, Saudi Arabia**

*This Egyptian student said he's going to do my flyer idea in Saudi Arabia. I said that would be fantastic. He said he thinks many young people would call a "secret ear."*

**Kate, 26, Maryland (301-651-XXXX)**

I'm not a size 0 and I have a lot of tats, even though I work a corporate job....I'm not Paris Hilton, skinny bitch. It's hard to get a date.

**Ashley**

I'm in the library making copies of my resume....I just ordered The Lover on interlibrary loan.

**Martha, 22 (573-825-XXXX)**

Still no job :(

**706-888-XXXX**

Why do bad relationships suck so bad?

**Valerie (973-283-XXXX)**

I'm prone to panic attacks.

**602-330-XXXX**

Yeah, have fun at work.

*Kira became my full-time job. When the doctors wouldn't give Kira a new prescription for Klonopin, because she used the last one too quickly, we'd go to Bellevue, the psychiatric ward. In the seven months we were together, we went to Bellevue at least three times. My acting, writing, and stand-up comedy career went on hiatus.*

**Young woman, barista**

I can't find the courage to quit....I'm angry at myself, though, because I don't want to waste time doing something I don't want to do....I'm working at Starbucks but only till the end of the year so I can save up some money and go on a trip.

## Liam, Air Force officer (860-942-XXXX)

I joined the military in 1992 and became an officer through the ROTC college program....I met my wife in the Air Force. She quit when she became pregnant. We were very loving and solid until 9/11....I was deployed all over the world without much warning. I was hardly ever home. She eventually filed for divorce....She got full custody of the kids and I'm paying child support....I got screwed. It's made me bitter. She had me arrested for harassment and now she's trying to turn my kids against me.

## 978-476-XXXX

Yeah, what do you want to save the world from?... I just feel hopeless at times....That's what I like to do....Have you ever felt like you aren't going to amount to anything?... That's cool....I just wonder if I'm ever going to be something, you know?... I'm a sad person.... It takes awhile to bounce back from something like that, man....My name's Hank, by the way....Indeed...I think I'm going to be a guidance counselor....Does that sound like a helpful occupation?

## Scott, 33, Wisconsin (920-784-XXXX)

After I did 9 years in the military, I worked as an X-ray tech at a trauma center. I lost my faith in humanity there, seeing trauma every night. Innocent people always coming in dying. Someone gets hit by a drunk driver, shot by a thief. Hard stuff, man. I drank a 12-pack a night. I broke down finally when this homeless guy came in. He had lice in his dreadlocks so bad that he put ethyl alcohol all over his dreads and then lit a cigarette. Poof. I used to do one-hitters in the parking lot during breaks.

77

**24-year-old medical student, Michigan**

I love to party....Nearly died in Cancun from alcohol poisoning.

**NYC man, studying to be doctor (646-610-XXXX)**

You got me thinking about my own issues.

**Anitchka**

I like men, but I joke about liking women....Why? Do I look like a lesbian?

**Devon, 24 (774-444-XXXX)**

Not sure exactly, maybe counseling...I graduated a couple years ago with a psych degree....I get attacked nearly every shift, feces thrown at me, try to punch my face out....Yeah, it's the graveyard shift at an adult home for the mentally ill and disabled....The one prison I worked at was mostly lifers, so they were needy for your attention.

**201-783-XXXX**

What would you do if someone you don't know starts texting you, asking for personal info, and then starts calling you names?

*Trauma has altered my brain chemistry. You can give me 1,000 pills and nothing's changing me.*

**920-543-XXXX**

Are you mean or nice?

**856-973-XXXX**
I try my hardest to be nice, but people take advantage of me and stomp all over me.

**Doug**
What's your opinion on religion?

**707-348-XXXX**
I go door to door talking about solar panels.

**407-535-XXXX**
I'm the Minister of Depression.

**703-517-XXXX**
I miss you, Jeff.

**Girls' volleyball team, Illinois**
We lost tournament & need 2 vent...Ur r ear.

**18-year-old girl, senior, starter on basketball team (217-720-XXXX)**
Jeff, I have a cast on my hand....I got an injury playing basketball....Can I still play basketball with a cast?

**Erica**
Sprained ankle...Have to stay home next 3 days...I miss you.

**954-673-XXXX**
Feeling fat and not good enough.

**Erica**

My collarbones are really weird.

**250-318-XXXX**

Currently bored because my foot's broken and I can't go any-where....Oh wow. Sorry about your breakup....It sounds like a cool experiment....Sounds stimulating....Probably better than my job... I'm a shoe salesman....Just saving up to move to Vancouver.... You'd have a different opinion if you met my boss.

**309-721-XXXX**

You're a genuine 50-year-old prick, aren't you? Leave me the fuck alone!

**Ashley**

I am at my horniest point of the month right now....I'm dying for dick. I'm all swollen and can't keep my hands off myself.

**Bethany (845-282-XXXX)**

The gym I work at is a meat market. I'm a receptionist there while working for my degree in finance....I love to eat. I spend all my money on food....Mostly burgers and steaks. So yeah, I need to work out a lot.

**Valerie (973-283-XXXX)**

He doesn't eat normal, either. He only eats fat-free foods, and if I tell him I feel guilty about having eaten, he says, "Well, maybe you shouldn't have had that muffin," but what I want him to say is, "It's ok." I need to go to the gym.

**Erica**
Actually, I'm really ugly. Sorry.

**720-224-XXXX**
I'm online and just found a picture that was way too true. One side of the picture had an empty room that said number of people who find me attractive. On the other side was a huge crowd of people and it said number of people who find my best friend attractive.

**347-620-XXXX**
It's a modeling job and I have to give a speech to get the job.... Thanks. I'm great with giving speeches, but for some reason whenever I have to talk about myself, I freak out.

*I was sitting in my room last month with Kira. I was thinking seriously about killing myself. Maybe I'm schizophrenic. I've thought that on numerous occasions. I felt as if I were waking up and had no idea how I got there.*

**512-553-XXXX**
Drama with my girlfriend, or ex. Idk what to call her. Not really drama either, just confusing shit, mixed signals...It's ridiculous. Strips for me on Skype. Then gets all closed off the next day.

**Krystal**
It's no big deal, but I'm a girl, a teenage girl, so I get emotional.

**Kira**

Wish I was different...That I didn't feel so much...I'm cursed.... Sorry that you once loved me....Wish I was different.

**Jacqueline, 31, Ohio (224-622-XXXX)**

I wish I was different too....Why?... I'm suicidal. Full of melancholy. And hatred...No, I don't love myself at all....I hate myself actually, but love all my friends....The broad picture is even worse. I'm grateful for shit....I have nothing to live for....Can't make a gratitude list... Fuck Tony Robbin....My day sucks. I forgot my crew clothes and I'm just a total wreck....I overslept.

**305-773-XXXX**

Im sleepy. And talking nonsense.

**Hector (224-622-XXXX)**

I need a sex partner....I know, easier said than done.

**404-917-XXXX**

I effin' hate eating....Makes me feel like a fatty.

**Man, Jupiter, Florida**

How did you get through this? Isolation can make you homicidal.

**716-548-XXXX**

I'm making gingerbread houses, so call back later.

*I just don't want to feel weird anymore. I love and miss Kira and need to live in a nice house with her. I figured out I need my own office/room and that I need to be alone in the mornings, just working on my stuff, having my own time. Hopefully I will just be able to write and act soon!*

**917-701-XXXX**
What are you writing about?

**917-945-XXXX**
I have to write logs for gym....Can I pretend I did soccer with you or something lol?

**Kira (September)**
am i your story?

**Girl, 18, New York University student (440-935-XXXX)**
Tell me about your book. I want to know everything about you!

**Marissa (517-526-XXXX)**
Yeah, if you happen to like the kinds of things I do....Have you read *Extremely Loud and Incredibly Close*?... For some reason your sign made me think of the book, but I'm not sure why.

**584-246-XXXX**
Feel bad I haven't been reading a lot lately. It used to be one of my escapes.

**Jefferson, Missouri (769-257-XXXX)**
That sign of yours could be me. Same name, same feeling...I'm bored watching TV and on the internet. I sit around lonely. I lost

my job. Company went out of business...I'm not happy with the relationship business. It's not going well....Did you know that dildos are illegal in my town? We're in the Bible Belt. Funniest thing is to watch the police bust a porno shop....Well, I got to go. I'm going to McDonald's. Probably the only thing I'll do today besides watch TV.

### Erica

Well, dinner's over....The weirdest thing just happened actually.... I'm only half full. I still feel some kind of emptiness....I know this sounds really weird....But like whenever I see a bug or rodent, I just can't kill them. Not because I'm some pet activist or anything.... Sorry, that was really stupid. Never mind....Animals are so cute, especially puppies....Someone had to bathe me yesterday....And I cried...Because I became too disgusted with the idea of looking at myself, because I'm a disgrace. I'm always needing something and wanting something more. And it hurts and I can't do it anymore.... Yes, I am. I'm sorry. I just have these breakdowns....I hate being a downer. I want to lose a few pounds....I can't do that. I can barely look into a mirror. I can't gain weight and look at myself.... If I'm not a skeleton then I presume I'm humongous....I need to stop being a bitch and go with the flow....My body disgusts me and I don't care anymore....I resent him so much sometimes....He says I have angel eyes....He's cheated on me 3 times and I still don't know why I'm with him....I'm going to rest now....I feel terrible.... He never apologizes....Well I went to Connecticut and there was a lot of snow so basically I just took shots of that... And black and white. I don't like the smell of developing liquid though....Mostly I just do photography for fun and maintaining sanity....I'm not sure if I should go or not?... I don't think there's anything you could

do anyways....I never like deer, they are always so confused....
Ha ha...I think the moon's particularly glowing today, don't you?...
I don't want to kill myself but I don't understand my purpose of
being....Nice to know there's someone out there like me....Or is it
nice?... I'm not quite sure. It's a gift and a curse....I like the effects
I gave myself in the photo....I actually do look disgustingly obese in
this....I've tried to date other people, and they say I'm like a deer
caught in the headlights and I just don't know what I want or where
I'm going and they want someone who's sure of something and I'm
not....I never am....I'd tell you but you'd probably hate me....I can't
bear being myself....I look at my breasts and I look at my face and
my stomach....I starve myself....When I bathe sometimes I take a
razor and cut very deeply into my leg....And just sometimes I prick
myself with rose thorns.

**Amber (504-333-XXXX)**
Fine, I don't exist. I don't exist! I'm a ghost to you, right?

**646-460-XXXX**
Most of the time my dreams are annoying.

**949-813-XXXX**
I have an artistic soul and the people around me have less imagina-
tion than a brick. I don't mean to sound so cruel, but it's Orange
County. Land of fake breasts and spray tans.

**Brigette**
Been practicing my region flute music cause tryouts are this weekend.

## Katrina, 19, Missouri (573-825-XXXX)

I love going to concerts and playing video games....I was fired from Wal-Mart today. I'm a cashier and they asked me to do stock. I don't do stock. I said I couldn't do that. They said, "You're fired."... I'm jobless.

## Erica

I used to model and then I stopped eating, and I got heavily interested in art....You get one artistic person in the family and you're treated like a black sheep....Well, a lot of people think I look nice because I'm skinny. I've been anorexic. But now when I'm stressed with art and stuff, not eating helps....Yeah, sometimes I want to kill myself. Because, like, I don't understand...Kind of melancholy. Remembering my past.

## 917-544-XXXX

Meh, I just saw an exhibition at the brooklyn museum i could've lived without seeing....It said, "Adult Material" so I thought to myself, nice. More fap material. (I apologize for being so vulgar.)....I walk in and it's a bunch of dicks and trannys.

## Katrina

Cumming too fast happens to the best of them, Jeff, don't feel bad.

## Randi (616-821-XXXX)

Um lol hun I do so like talking to you but I recently lost my contacts and I'm not fully aware who I'm talking to.

**Peter (856-359-XXXX)**
But what if I don't know what my true character and identity is?

**Brittany**
Busy making myself feel worthless...Because that's just how screwed up I am. Like I need more friends with benefits.

**440-935-XXXX**
I don't fuck with that shit. It ended up that he has a gf named Caroline.

**Jonah (224-441-XXXX)**
I'm in class. There's a girl I dated in here and it gets awkward.

**Kimberly**
Do you hate me?

**Rhonda**
No. You're amazingly perfect. I'm a wreck. I kind of need to be held.

**817-879-XXXX**
Are you a robot?

**502-387-XXXX**
You should change your name to Felon....You look as homicidal and crazy as Willem Dafoe....Would it kill you to smile?

**540-819-XXXX**
Sometimes I wear a broken smile.

**Lucy**

Incredibly horny…You wanna sext?

**Erica**

I'm too fragile. You wouldn't like me much.

**781-724-XXXX**

What are you?

**Erica**

I'm sounding psychotic right now.

**Kirk**

That's just the way I roll….Leave a message, dick.

**213-854-XXXX**

I wish you could adopt me.

**Ricky**

Writtttttte me a poeeemm

**Tamara**

im in english…huckleberry finn. i hate it….im tired and depressed, as usual.

**Glen**

I was almost an English major. What do you write?

**616-560-XXXX**

I actually have no idea what I want to do. I hope I find what I have a passion for.

**Eliza**

I'm trying to finish a couple poems to send into a contest right now.

**NYU student (440-935-XXXX)**

I want to write something nasty. Dirty. Gritty and sexual. Not this bs!

**786-468-XXXX**

Ironically I actually saw your little ad with my gf. May I ask why it didn't work out with your gf?

*Kira would get extremely violent and start hitting me, saying the worst things. Things like she was glad my parents were dead. She'd rip on my dead parents, even though she'd never met them. She'd tell me I have the smallest dick she's ever seen.*

**Jorge**

Yeah I know how that feels. Hard to connect with people outside of your circle in this city.

**Claire and Georgia**

Why is it so hard to meet people in New York?

*A girlfriend of mine was an atheist, and she cheated on me. I know she probably rationalized it by thinking, "What he doesn't know won't hurt him." She really messed me up. I had to leave New York City for over a year, just to get away from her. I ended up in Mexico, coked out of my mind.*

## Monica (939-639-XXXX)
It's hot here in Puerto Rico!

## Isabella, 20, NYC (407-892-XXXX)
My friend got high and made out with another girl. We want to know if you think she's bi? Are all women bi?

## Kimberly
I'm so confused....I have no idea what you are trying to say to me....Me and my moods?...I can easily argue the same thing about you....You drive me wild with your mood swings!

*Kira was smoking and I could tell she'd been drinking. We talked and got into her van and drove down Riverside Drive. We found a spot somewhere in the 70s, where we were going to sleep for the night. A few minutes later, we were arguing and I stepped out of the van to take a piss. I was still half asleep. I said something negative about her acting. It was a cheap shot. As I was peeing outside the passenger door, she punched me as hard as she could in the back of my head. It almost knocked me over. I spun around without even thinking and hit her back. I know it sounds like I'm trying to get out of it. I'm not. It was truly a reflex. I didn't even think about it. It split her chin. I knew if we went to the hospital I'd get arrested.*

**Ashley**

That's a terrible breakup. I hope you're not thinking about hurting yourself.

**Brittany**

Grr. My bra is being uncooperative.

**305-773-XXXX**

What's a crazy weekend?

**347-879-XXXX**

Oh don't threaten me with a good time Jeff.

**702-278-XXXX**

Do you like pirates or ninjas?

# VI. Solutions

**Benji**
We came up with a few options of what you could do about being a lonely guy. You go out, find a party, a friend, anything, or you can stay home and masturbate and become sexually enlightened to your hand. Peace out, buddy.

**Starbucks employee**
Haha. I'm a dancer, so when I'm not working I'm doing that.

**Doreen (703-509-XXXX)**
Hey, Jeff. We're at Rockwood Music Hall. Come on down!

**215-545-XXXX**
I just heard my friend's band play at Barnard and saw your ad....The band was good....What was the movie you saw about?

**Morgan (818-223-XXXX)**
Thought of you in the shower.

**949-813-XXXX**
The best thing is to have your friends and not be reminded of her.

**Brittany**

Well my friend is currently in the bathroom taking a shower and that would require a mirror so I can't at the moment....You know, I can help you jack off without a picture. I'm very good with the imagination.

**786-564-XXXX**

I love dragons so much!

**Margaret (440-373-XXXX)**

I didn't teach you anything about happiness or forgiveness. I just reminded you of what you already knew.

**Luis**

I feel disconnected in general....I want to keep in contact with ya....I feel ya, man....Everyone does.

**920-543-XXXX**

Then we can be friends!

**Man at General Atomics, California (760-388-XXXX)**

What's the farthest call you've gotten?... Holy Christ!

**Erica**

Look at the moon....I hope the universe is treating you well, Jeff.

**212-470-XXXX**

And may the force be with you, Luke.

**Ardis (601-720-XXXX)**
Gotta get welding, but if you ever need to talk, feel free.

**970-433-XXXX**
Save me in your phone as Taco!!!!!!

**Rocky (828-775-XXXX)**
Have you ever sexted?

**Candice (408-230-XXXX)**
I like to be busy. When I'm bored, I tend to get myself into trouble.

**Krystal**
But I want to be with you. I would like you to become my best friend and then meet you and then date you and then be your girlfriend and then possibly marriage.

**Jack**
I'll get through it—mind over matter right?

**Daphne (940-595-XXXX)**
Hot wings and chocolate :)

**Serena**
Ah, the simple joy of a menthol Camel.

**Warren (956-984-XXXX)**
I'm about to smoke a blunt.

**Erica**

I fell asleep on a lump of gigantic stuffed animals at Toys R Us.

**250-709-XXXX**

Very nice. I'm at work right now (Subway) and I'm about to fall asleep!... I like the BLT and the Roasted Chicken.

**619-852-XXXX**

Hey jeff—you busy?... I'm bored....I'm just eating and talking to people....You're one of the people I'm talking to.

**720-470-XXXX**

Jeff? Would you like to meet up for coffee today? I'm Deborah.

**REI**

Jeff, hey, this is the REI team, and we just wanted to give you a call because we saw your flyer on a pole in front of our REI store on Lafayette Street. We just thought we'd invite you to come down here to REI and check out the store. It's for people who love the great outdoors, who are social, who love to talk, and apparently you love to talk and we don't want you to be lonely. "REI" stands for "recreational," "equipment," "incorporated."

**Krystal**

I've never met a guy like you before....I would be good to you....I wouldn't cheat....I am young. But will get older...In Washington if they are older than 16, and have consent, then it's ok....That's just in Washington, though. I don't know about New York and I don't want to get you arrested....I love you.

**English major, Pacific University, Forest Grove, Oregon (877-722-XXXX)**
Who doesn't love Francis Bacon?!

*At the age of 45, Bacon married a 14-year-old.*

**224-622-XXXX**
I wanna be your melody, going through your head when you think of me. I wanna be your favorite song, you can turn me up play me all night long. Lalalalalalalala.

**Max (254-592-XXXX)**
What kind of music do you like? I'm a metal head.

**Hannah**
Mostly black metal and 80s coldwave, minimal electronics.

**NYU student (440-935-XXXX)**
So Im not particularly girly like these fuckheads at NYU I meet.

**917-205-XXXX**
There's something oddly comforting to know I can say whatever to you and you won't have any real bias.

**Susan, 30, Long Island**
*Sociology major. Called from a noisy bar. Grew up on Long Island and worked as a graphic designer for years. Said she's going to do a study of drugs in America and post her number on a flyer. She became pretty annoying and kept*

*telling me to mail her any material I had from my phone calls that involved drugs. She's the only person I hung up on out of thousands.*

**Musician (715-250-XXXX)**
Jeff you are a badass.

**Bruce (321-961-XXXX)**
I have an urge to poke you in the kidney. Hard.

**917-855-XXXX**
Peace man...You wanna come smoke with us?

**402-541-XXXX**
Good morning and happy hump day, mister Jeff.

**617-784-XXXX**
We're making french fries.

**Ashley**
I'm joining the Coast Guard.

*Picture of Ashley's smiling face and naked, robust breasts. Picture message: "Somehow, I fear basic training's gonna trim these puppies down."*

**Air Force pilot, Spain**
I'm flying missions to Libya....Be confident with the women.... That's what they like.

*The pilot sends me pictures before a Halloween sortie; he and his copilot are dressed in clown suits.*

**910-759-XXXX**
Hey, I'm great. Just chillin in Holland for the year.

**Ashley**
Sorry that took awhile. I had to give my baby sister a bath....She's excited for her birthday tomorrow....Excellent birth control...But the baby's so cute.

**323-774-XXXX**
Sorry it took a while. I was in us history. I'm in 11th grade.

**973-283-XXXX**
Thanks for telling me u think im intelligent. it's one of the most meaningful compliments you can give....ur helping a lot of ppl and probably earning urself lots and lots of good karma :)

**Ashley**
I love my old school Carl Sagan. Nothing better than a healthy dose of existential physics to make your mind spin before bed.

**Goldman Sachs trader**
It's weird no one has done what you have in the last 50 years or so since the phone's been in most households. Anyone could've done it.

**626-664-XXXX**
You're awesome. We love you.

**708-381-XXXX**

I'm watching nova. U?

**Car salesman, 40, Route 66, New Jersey**

In the short term, drink a lot. Long term, it just takes time, man.

**Erica**

Apparently I really fucked myself up this time. I'm supposed to be drinking a crapload of fluids from now on, and I'm not doing that. I could care less about whether I die or not.

**Ashley**

I feel that way too. I usually have the whole existential crisis experience once a year.

**972-616-XXXX**

Not a whole lot…Working on some French and making a sandwich…Turkey and cheese…Nothing special with mayo and mustard on wheat.

**Laticia, 33, Florida (386-453-XXXX)**

I found the smallest turkey, so me and the cat are going to have a nice dinner on Thanksgiving. Not a lot of fixings.

**780-667-XXXX**

We celebrate in October in Canada, but I'll make some stuffing tonight anyways for you.

## 970-623-XXXX
I'm eating a hotdog....How is your burrito?

## Ashley
You eat me out. I come over and over.

## Girl, college student, NYU
I ate one of those waffles you make in the griddle thingy. I like to eat the batter. But today it was a lil gritty and didn't have enough vanilla.

## Second marine in California
I missed flapjacks and American butter the most....First stop after returning from Honduras, and getting out of the hospital, was IHOP.

## 801-376-XXXX
Sweetdreams and wetdreams Lonely Jeff

## 276-870-XXXX
I weigh myself backwards at the doctor's office. He has to weigh me bimonthly because of my eating disorder. I have to do it backwards, because if I look at my weight, it ruins my day.

## 347-858-XXXX
I'm exploring my bi-curiosity.

## Erica
Honestly, I think my soul is hungry.

**718-666-XXXX**

We'll have a drink sometime.

**Anitchka**

Anyone is capable of committing suicide....I promise I won't, though.

**Olivia**

But when my boyfriend asks my weight, I refuse to tell him.

**715-771-XXXX**

This is from Cooper. I love you. That is all.

**Raymond**

Life is great. Put a smile on your face. Someone out there wants you to smile! Bye, Jeff...Have a great day.

**Gabriel**

I don't just enjoy the weekends. I enjoy every day!... My days are different than most....I give historical tours of bars of New York.... I've been to rehab 3 times....It only gets better.

**512-569-XXXX**

Well today I got stoned outta my mind and am now eating bugles for my munchies.

**801-557-XXXX**

We should go to Africa together, mate.

## 718-910-XXXX

It's a big world out there though, Lonely Guy Jeff, and there are friendships to be found on every street corner!... May I suggest a book club?... Maybe take up an activity like bowling....What you say?

## 787-518-XXXX

Sorry, I was in a conference....It was about monkeys and I'm gonna work with them!... Tell me about yourself.

## Marcus, 58, Queens (917-215-XXXX)

I don't tend to know everything about the human condition, but you are lonely, the flyer reads, is that correct?... Ok then. When it's sunny, the farthest thing you can see is the sun. When it's dark, you can see farther, much farther....Great works derive from genuine despair....It allows one to see things inside other people and one-self clearer. I've helped a few people out in my life....I'm just lucky I haven't been in a situation where I've had to kill people to survive. Let's get together next week, I will pass on wisdom gained from others....Great ideas outlast us all.

## 805-407-XXXX

My dad got me a new laptop so I love him now.

*Gay man wants to send me nude photos.*

## Man, 50, South Carolina

Want Foo Fighter tix? Female friend sitting next to u...Be strong before entering a relationship....Buy precious metals.

**Bret**

Hey, me and my girlfriend are on Houston Street....What do you think about buying a co-op in this current real estate market?

*I told Bret to buy—the market is at the bottom.*

**Office worker**

How did I get over it? I got married.

**Tracey (804-539-XXXX)**

Yeah, one of my best friends completely betrayed me and that was hurtful. I've been seeing a therapist, though, and she's made me feel a lot better.

**23-year-old woman from New Orleans (504-333-XXXX)**

I met my boyfriend through mutual friends. I'd just gotten out of a bad relationship and really wasn't into meeting someone else, but I said, "Ok, I'll go out to dinner. I could gain one more friend." We hit it off....We've been together for 6 months and I'm incredibly happy.

**Man, 65, Upper West Side**

Write gratitude lists.

**Thelma, 15, Oklahoma (918-313-XXXX)**

I met Randy in computer technology class....His best friend asked me to be in their project group....I said yes we hung out at teen club and that's all she wrote.

## First marine in California

Awesome! I find writers are the unsung heroes of the English language. My friend Chris in London writes for a prestigious museum out there.

*I was looking around and thinking I have absolutely nothing. The only hope I have is an essay I'm hoping to publish next year.*

## Three women, Buffalo art gallery (716-833-XXXX)

We're drinking wine and eating cheese and talking about you and we've decided your project should be a Cubist-type book.... It's so different....We can meet and talk when we visit NYC in December.

## Charmaine, Brooklyn

Are you black?

## Brittany

Conflicted. But that's just normal for me I suppose.

## Ryan

You look nothing like I thought. I thought you'd be short, fat, and have curly long hair.

## Chuck

Obviously it didn't work out with you and Kira. You wanna switch teams?

**Alyssa**

I don't have anything else to do.

**Denver girl, 21 (303-217-XXXX)**

I was home alone so I got drunk and did magic. It was pretty sad.... You stay up till dawn when you drink sometimes?... People here like to wake up stupid early and watch the sunrise from lookout mountain.

**720-984-XXXX**

That sucks. Need to talk about it?... I'm just chilling at home all day. Might play some Xbox, might clean house if I get really bored. Probably gonna watch some Southpark too.

**MK (646-755-XXXX)**

You'll be ok....Bless you, Jeff....You've already accomplished great things despite your losses and bumps in life....Turning in for 2nite.

**Jenny (517-366-XXXX)**

I'm really exhausted....I'm going back to sleep for now....I'll text you when I wake up.

**Ashley**

Morning sex. It's my favorite. You could come at me from behind. I love how deep that is. It makes me moan every time your dick hits my cervix.

**JH (224-766-XXXX)**

I like this friendship we've created.

**Mike**

Join an organization and meditate.

*Three homosexuals partying in SoHo want me to join them.*

**Man in Chinatown**

I need information to find best activities for you.

**Jennifer (212-775-XXXX)**

You're a Navy Seal.

**618-420-XXXX**

Lying in bed with my friend.

**Arkansas man**

I'm calling to offer support.

**Jessie (256-503-XXXX)**

Hey, I realize you've probably had an influx of people calling and texting you. I just wanted to say thanks. If more people were just there
to listen to people, the world would be a better place.

**Caleb, Arkansas (870-489-XXXX)**

Things are really good here! Already partying at 10 am! What's
going on, man? The beer's exceptionally good!

**224-622-XXXX**

I'm happy today. My teacher's a bitch and she's not here. We have
Mr. Crocker sub.

**Melinda, 54, therapist, breast cancer survivor, Corvallis, Oregon**
You've hit on something in the collective. Reflection is the key to learning. Anything is possible. My odds of survival were ice thin. I'm alive, happy, and still learning.

**Danielle, eastern Long Island**
I dropped out of school today, am sick of it.

**616-957-XXXX**
Actually it's more I'm motivated than super smart. I mean I failed the last 3 years of school, then I came to this alternative school and now I'm getting all A's.

*Brian Quinn called from set of his TV show, Impractical Jokers. He put some of the stars of the show on the phone.*

**Brittany**
I can't get that image of me pinning you down, grinding my slick pussy up and down the underside of your cock, out of my head.

**423-483-XXXX**
How exactly was Andrew Jackson like Napoleon?... I guess the lesson here is that anyone can build up from nothing. That we can all repair, need be...I'll look for that bio on Jackson....They both came from nothing? Fair enough....But wasn't Napoleon a general first?... Gotcha. They both should've failed.

**16-year-old high school boy**
Illinois is boring. I'm moving to LA to be a movie star.

**502-387-XXXX**
I dig Clockwork Orange. You remind me of a Clockwork Orange with your off-beat meanderings and tumultuous rants, oh my brothers. I'd love to vetch a devotchka real horrorshow with ya, Jeff. A lil of the ole in-out, in-out, ultraviolent, eh? A lil vetchyvetchy with some devotchkas, no? Oh, my brothers and sisters, how I love orgies and saucy devotchkas slicked river-high of broken dreams! JD all over their bodies, coke on their asses.

**Maddy (702-782-XXXX)**
Yeah, I know. Am going in the same way rite now :/

**Pete (401-644-XXXX)**
I'm an upper. Think of me as your speed.

**Glenna, California (925-289-XXXX)**
Meditate and you reach Nirvana and your aura will be blue instead of red.

**917-361-XXXX**
You better not have cheated!

*Woman, Michigan, divorced, two kids. Studying nursing. Not lonely.*

**519-859-XXXX**
Apparently they do care about you, Jeff. That's really cool.

**517-526-XXXX**

I've been there before, bro. Chin up!... I just hit the 1-year anniversary of my finance leaving me....It's been a rough road, but I'm finally starting to get my life back on track.

**Delilah, 33 (415-320-XXXX)**

W/ a group of producers...We're doing a feature in San Francisco....We're bored, even though we're extremely busy....Your "journey" should be a film.

**860-331-XXXX**

I have to go. The bus is going to blow up.

**Girl**

I'm home. You can stop worrying about me making it safely, my guardian angel.

**Joaquin (305-799-XXXX)**

I got a new shiatsu, Barney. We go to the dog park. When I tell Barney that that woman's hot he really turns the charm on, wagging the tail. Barney's helping me meet beautiful women.

**607-873-XXXX**

Jeff! I love you Jeff!

**Tyrone**

Really, Jeff?...Mental health services through the state?...All right, yeah, I'll try it.

## 707-362-XXXX

Wtf is wrong with you dude? You need to go to a mental hospital.

## Ashley

Beg pardon? I'm taking my aunt out today. She lives in a group home for the mentally disabled. She's a doll.

## Woman, 24, studied for 2 years in Israel (704-516-XXXX)

What's the difference between a surgeon and a pilot? We do research to see if the surgeon's competent. We check out his record, his success rate. We don't check out an airline pilot's safety record. We trust that he flies safely. The surgeon performs the surgery and goes home. There's a chance you could die in surgery, but the surgeon still goes home. The pilot goes down with the plane. We're all in this life together. All humans are together. If you ever need someone to talk to, call me. If you crash, the pilot crashes.

## Man at General Atomics

We build the planes....If you're ever in California, Lonely Jeff, and want a plane ride, look us up.

## Liam

I should be promoted to colonel next year and then I can retire with full pension in 5 years. Even though my ex is trying to fuck me over, the pension should be enough to help me put my kids through college....Keep your head up, meet people, and live happily.

**Jim, 30, lumberjack, Maine (260-415-XXXX)**

Keep on keepin' on. You want work, Jeff, we'll put ya ta work springing trees or splittin' wood in the mill. You won't be lonely no more.... I'm hitting the club tonight. Only got a couple around here, so it's slim pickins. Keep on keepin' on.

**Javier**

I thought about our conversation and came to the conclusion I was quite selfish and narcissistic. I never asked you about anything. So tell me about yourself, Jeff.

**Amy**

You ready to go to a swingers' party?

**Mick, 45**

If you want to get away with an armored car heist, this works, trust me. Get an excessively good-looking woman, hottest babe you can find. Pay her to wear nothing. Then have her walk by the armored car right when they swing the door open for a drop. As the guards are staring at her tits, throw a smoke bomb into the car and grab a bag of cash and run....Successful armored car heists happen often, Jeff. They go unreported for good reason.... You can get away with a few bank heists. First couple, cinch. They don't expect the hit. After that, either plan well or you're doing a 7-year stretch....Disguises for crimes are underrated. Most people who wear disguises are very successful with baby felonies.

**Paige (347-620-XXXX)**
Who is this?... Omg I had you saved in my phone with my boy-friend's name!!!!!

*Paige then "accidentally" sent me her photo and a quick text: "Sorry went to wrong person."*

**501-208-XXXX**
Dude, I would totally be your wingman if I was there with you.

**224-622-XXXX**
You're a pretty chill guy.

**Howie, 26, law student, Arkansas (501-269-XXXX)**
I don't date much. Been there, done that...I want to be a prosecutor because there's lots of injustice and craziness out there. Hardly any-one got busted for Enron....Financial swindlers should be treated like crack dealers—same animals.

**Thelma (918-313-XXXX)**
Everyone says Randy's my everything....He has such a sweet heart....I love him to death.

*The image that entered my mind was me pulling a gun out in Riverside Park, putting the barrel in my mouth, and shooting myself in front of Kira.*

**Ashley**
Then we change locations, we're in an alley or bathroom. You feel me up, I blow you, and you pull my hair.

**Katrina**
The guy I was with last night kept pulling my hair and telling me what to do, hehe.

**347-858-XXXX**
I hope everyone is keeping you distracted nicely.

**503-318-XXXX**
No, sir. I'm a hairdresser.

**Garrett**
Everyone loves you. I looked you up on Google. You're a phenomenon!

*Three girls on a tour bus; one guy. Guy got on and talked about his new contacts.*

**Katrina**
Last night I had a one-night stand....Today I got new frames for my lenses.

*Some guy calls and says, "Hey, is this Lonely Jeff?" I say, "Yes." He says, "Get a girl, man," hangs up.*

**817-681-XXXX**

My nickname's Chica.

**904-469-XXXX**

Sex is for unstressing.

**Kelsey**

Well my blood tests all came back good, so I'm clear to go back to work.

**High school girl, Florida (347-549-XXXX)**

I love animals and want to work for the Humane Society. Before, when we were living in New York, there was a wounded white dove on the ledge outside our apartment. I caught it and fed it bread for 3 days until it got better and then let it go.

*This Florida high school girl's voice is filled with laughter, innocence, and curiosity. She reminds me of a character in a Salinger story.*

**352-857-XXXX**

Nigga, you don't know me.

**217-954-XXXX**

You're nerd famous, that's awesome.

**636-544-XXXX**

I'm just writing about life.

**Jenna**

I have a lot to say and I should be a writer but have nothing but one liners and I tend to type how I speak.

**Steve**

Has anyone ever asked: Was Kennedy wearing a seatbelt?

**Taylor**

I'm riding horses this weekend. I really miss the barn. I'm looking forward to volunteer work at the barn, even mucking stalls. It relaxes and frees me. Yoga with an odor.

**646-884-XXXX**

I suggest a tour of the largest garbage dump in the world. It's so close, Staten Island. The garbage dump's been closed for 10 years. The smell has been preserved as if it closed yesterday. I'm sure you'll leave with a different outlook on life.

**Paige (2 days before our first date)**

If you think I'm hideous and don't want to meet, that's fine....You do? Really?... Ok, see you on Thursday.

**Man speaking very slowly (860-460-XXXX)**

Jeffrey...Jeffrey...Jeffrey...Jeffrey...

**617-921-XXXX**

You should detox your soul.

# VII. No God Created This Mess

*I'm pretty sure one man who called was a serial killer. He was very standoffish. He said, "I didn't know if I should call. You could be a serial killer." That's all he talked about. Of course his number was blocked. He said, "What if a serial killer called a serial killer who posted an ad like yours, then they tried to kill each other?" He said maybe a serial killer would come after me. I said let him try. I said I'm not scared of dying.*

**Man, Las Vegas**
I'm not afraid of living or dying. I'm afraid of *not* living.

**330-323-XXXX**
Hooray internet! Best way to make friends.

**845-548-XXXX**
I think you've done a beautiful thing....As much as it has helped you, you have helped the world so much more. Good karma can change everything....I would love to be brave enough to put myself out there like that. The best advice is always advice from the perspective I've never seen it from....Perhaps a different, caring stranger will be the one who you end up with in the long run.

**305-773-XXXX**

The homie sounds questionable.

**540-471-XXXX**

Just in case you yourself are an axe murder I would like you to know my phone is untraceable and I know Brazilian Jiu-Jitsu....None of that is true.

**Fashion photographer**

I'm a hired gun. I was a teacher, then I left to pursue photography. The fashion gigs are shallow, but they're good money.

*The photographer started crying.*

**Alison (646-258-XXXX)**

I once knew a photographer, Bruno Zehdnerha, who travelled to the Antarctic and photographed penguins. He created a penguin calendar. A blizzard took his life.

**Elaine**

Dad died of cancer. Mom has diabetes. My family is riddled with illnesses. I want to be a nurse who goes around the world so I can travel and heal.

**Erica**

You know the economy all over the world would go down drastically if human trafficking was stopped? I find it appalling that a large chunk of the world depends on the pain of families and the lives of others for profit. It makes me disgusted to be a human being even.

**Brittany**

Aw, poor thing…That makes sense, though. It takes an interesting kind of person to talk to random strangers just because they say they're lonely.

**Lauren, 25, Pennsylvania (717-579-XXXX)**

I was never a slut, but I did bring a lot of guys home just after graduating from college….Yeah, the sex was great….It left me empty….I got laid off from the marketing firm and my parents let me move back home to their awesome log cabin home….They're great people, hippies….I hated the business world. You make money in business by being deceptive….I want to be a nurse.

*Lauren is terribly intelligent and original, has the cutest laugh, and is physically attractive. Her texts kill.*

**Katrina**

Out of the 10 guys I've been with no one's been able to make me cum.

**Journalism student, 20 (313-969-XXXX)**

I live for drama and strife; that's why I want to travel and write profiles of interesting people….Maybe a war correspondent. There's drama there even when things are good.

**Anabelle (973-283-XXXX)**

He dumped me in this big blowout. It wasn't pretty….But my sister's an addict and she met this religious guy in Brooklyn and he changed her. She quit drugs, but she stopped talking to me and my family….

We haven't heard from her in months....Thank you...I think he was abusive too....My parents hired a PI to find her and he traced the guy's name to an apartment in the Bronx....No, the apartment was abandoned....The PI said that the landlord at his last place said the guy punched holes into the walls and had a violent history.

**Sandi (630-209-XXXX)**
I'd like to think you are the nice guy as advertised and not a serial killer.

*A guy I know named Mason told me he saw seven people get murdered in prison. He said when you want to kill someone, you coordinate four or five hits to go on at the same time, in different locations, so the guards are running everywhere and can't stop the murders. He also said if you want to kill someone with a shank, you aim for the third button down, the heart.*

**Holly, 22 (503-866-XXXX)**
Studying criminology...I want to be a homicide detective....Me and Sandy are driving from Alabama to Florida to party for Thanksgiving.

**541-232-XXXX**
Sometimes Thanksgiving just sucks giant naked monkey ass.

**Woman, 30, Wilmington, North Carolina**
We went crabbing today and then ate blue crabs with garlic and butter....Wilmington's full of fabulously wealthy people and college students....I'm going to a bar tonight with my girlfriend. She wants

to get married in a couple years. I'm on the fence....We couldn't get married in this state, too Bible Belt-y....Probably New York...Aren't you worried some crazy sociopath is going to come after you?

### Jackson (309-721-XXXX)
You look like the killer from Prom Night.

### Alexis, 37, Ohio
I was in a hospital for an eating disorder. You lose all rights. You are locked up in fact. You can't have jewelry because you might cut yourself. You can't even have a spiral notebook because that could be a weapon to harm yourself. I remember this stick-thin, 50-ish woman. Pretty, kind of a Marilyn Monroe quality, but a stick. At meals she'd say, "I'm a bad person. I shouldn't have eaten, but I had to do it. I had to finish my meal." True, the nurse would make us finish most of our food. I even had to finish my meal once after the woman across from me threw up in her plate. If you didn't eat, you didn't "move up levels" and you were stuck. I moved up rapidly and everyone was upset and jealous.

### 715-410-XXXX
You seem intelligent. Mind if I ask what you do for a living?

### Arnie, 42, Brooklyn
I was in the cage for 7 and change....Grand theft auto and a couple under-10 drug charges. I've been convicted 4 times....Started stealing at 10 for survival....I'll end up back in the joint...Because I got no education and I ain't going to be doing an 8-hour, pushing carts at Home Depot for some asshole with a minivan with a

cheating soccer wife....No, part of my parole and recovery is that I'm supposed to go to drug and AA meetings....You oughta see it. Everyone's miraculously saved by Jesus in these meetings until they kill their neighbor next week....No God created this mess. No God would give me the cards I got, man....You fuckin' serious? My dad was in prison, a lifer, for murder when I was 7. Mom couldn't raise us....I'll call again, J.

*Arnie sounded wildly exuberant, an adrenaline junkie jacked on some sauce.*

**832-622-XXXX**
Hey Jeff. This is God.

**Henrietta, 27, Texas (956-802-XXXX)**
I think a marriage with a prisoner might be the best. They can't hurt you as much as the dude in your bed who can torture you....I'm never my real self to people. I feel if I give them me in my entirety, I'll be vulnerable and then they'll have me at their fangs....He was cheating on me and I found out through friends; it was embarrassing and a psycho breakup....You know, it's funny—my uncle directs horror films....I'm studying neuroscience: the brain's outer space. In 50 years, I want to land on the moon....I love cold, windy, hopeless days, hot chocolate, and warm blankets....I'm worried I might end up in a mental institution. Too much goes on at times in my head.

**WG, 25, psychology degree (774-444-XXXX)**
I'm not going to do prison counseling....The one prison I worked at, the prisoners latch onto you and try to manipulate you into breaking

the rules for them....Like talking to people on the outside, sneaking messages into prison, that stuff...Family and friends had mostly abandoned them.

**Marsha (513-502-XXXX)**
I live in Ohio and I'm a junior in high school ha ha....What do you write? I think I want to write.

**Lacey (440-345-XXXX)**
U are different than I expected but still the same.

*Mom always liked Martin more than me. She liked wild people. Martin was always up for an adventure. Bungee jumping, skiing on avalanche runs. He was driving illegally at 13. I was the scared kid with sweaty hands who mumbled. I used to mumble practically every word. And I couldn't look anyone in the eye. That's still difficult. My grandma said she never felt hands so sweaty.*

**Ashley**
So smooth, Jeff. So smooth...How about soft love to start and frenzied fucking the 2nd go-around?

**Girl, NYU student (440-935-XXXX)**
Yes and no. What constitutes cozy? No, in that my hair's dripping onto my shoulders and the bed's shitty. Yes, in that I'm exhausted but have soft satin sheets.

**Victoria**

Right now i'm content, in general i'm stressed. :(

**Nanci (347-891-XXXX)**

R u ok do u need any assistance before i leave u?

**Kimberly**

You have to call me and tell me a bedtime story....Maybe. I'll take tons of pictures of you....You left me hanging yesterday and I couldn't sleep :(

**707-362-XXXX**

Are you just a computer program set to see how many people call or text a number they find on the internet?... What are you doing imitating a government program?

*I would estimate that around 50,000 people have called or texted so far.*

**Melissa**

I used to think I was philanthropic, but that was an internet phase.... Mom wanted a I eave It to Beaver family. I didn't fit the mold. I was a tomboy....We've got mental illness and criminals on both sides of the family....I love to make pies. I make a mean lasagna....I watch Netflix a lot. I'm not a huge lover of people in general.

**Erica**

And sometimes I believe I'm a mystery made for another world. I've told you about my dream of being washed in silver, haven't I?

Becoming the silver, becoming the moon, cosmic. Lunar. My soul shall leave and that's where it will go. The moon. And fill the craters with ideas and memories too complex for a universe yet basking in simplicity. I'll run my fingers along the lines and embrace the feelings of every being since the beginning of time. And before that. And just drown in the never ending slivers of faded light, an eternity of life.

**Helen**

I've always been interested in astronomy and geophysical science and the cycles of the moon, and I love tattoos, so I thought why not? I got the entire solar system on my back.

**540-471-XXXX**

I miss the city a lot, though, cow manure just isn't the same as smog.

**Jane Ann, 48, NYC (646-258-XXXX)**

I'm a lonely New Yorker too….I work in investment banking. People in my industry, well, Manhattan in general, are too busy for their own good. They aren't living….They work nonstop, go to dinner, a bar, a movie, then sleep. They wake up 20, 30 years later and realize they haven't lived. The city has a high suicide rate. Do the math. I get outside of it every weekend….Horse riding, hiking, trees, nature, I need the outdoors….It's funny, I have colleagues who ask how I can stand the smell of horses all weekend. Under my breath I respond, How can you stand being in this artificial environment all the time?… Same thing with dating. It's atrocious. The men act as if they're doing you a favor by being with you....I want to meet the man of my dreams.

*I'm going to meet Jane Ann for coffee.*

**Ashley**
Anyone who has lived in a pretty cow town has floated past so many ups and downs.

**Lilly (678-314-XXXX)**
Tomorrow's Thanksgiving and my grandma's having a cow because my room's not spotless....Cleaning my room, breaking things.

**Nathan**
Sorry, was clawing at the final frontiers of my perpetually messy apt...It seems like if I don't deal with the random piles of paper, the squalor regenerates by morning....Lazy. And/or shiftless. Oh! And feckless, of course...Say, are you really reaching out because you're lonely?... I've never felt lonely. Ever. I swear, I'm a freak in that way....But not being able to tell my best friend all the funny oddities that happen all day is perhaps a form of loneliness? Or aloneness? Not that that's a word....This is weird but interesting.... Sleep tight.

**Angela**
It's ok, dear....I don't sleep very well as it is, but thank you....I hope you're having an exciting, eventful day.

## Janie (347-755-XXXX)

Helluva day lost my wallet no subway money walked home...School sucks and I'm suckin' @ it....I will i will thx...No can't focus...Thanks i'll try not to beat myself up about it....I have to apply to college.

## 16-year-old girl, NYC

Harvard!...Cuz it's the best....Then any IVY league school...Maybe a lawyer or beta designer...Both my parents got GEDs and went to shitty community colleges....Mom's disabled....I love Poe!... I write poetry too.

*I'm meeting a French woman at Bowery Poetry Club. She called and we talked. She's a tall blonde.*

## Australian high school girls

Nicole Kidman is a bitch. We don't like her here....We're studying science and Indonesian....We ride kangaroos to school....We're in bikini tops and shorts. It's hot....We love you, Jeff!... What's your address? We want to send you something.

## Air Force pilot

I'm the guy in the Air Force who called from Spain. I told my friend to call you.

## Emily (646-258-XXXX)

Why text? Seems like the thing now, kind of stops real communication. Id rather speak in person. Texting seems so artificial.

**502-381-XXXX**
Would you like your phone number removed from reddit.com or are you cool with it?... I'm a moderator here....Not much. Smoking a doob and eating strawberry Oreos.

**502-387-XXXX**
Cool...This feels weird....I don't even know where to start.

**Kent**
Fresh out of the shower and nothing to do today.

**Cassandra (501-736-XXXX)**
Tomorrow's Tabby's birthday and I'm trying to finish her cake. She wanted a Scooby Doo-themed cake. It kind of turned out like Chewbacca. I am not a lady of culinary talents. It's delicious, albeit not appetizing.

**913-633-XXXX**
No problem...I love camping, reading, cooking....Anything but seafood...I don't hate it. I just swell up.

**Ashley**
Every time I exercise I feel that runner's high and feel fantastically in the mood to get drunk. Shit. It's 2:30. Can't do that.

**224-622-XXXX**
When I saw The Hangover on TV it didn't occur to me that it'd be censored.

## Jenna

My last name is Deadman.

*Jim Caviezel has told me I've had my share of suffering. He starred as Jesus in the movie* The Passion of the Christ. *He's a devout Catholic. Our families vacationed every summer for weeks at Spader Bay Resort in Lake Chelan. It was party central.*

## Valerie

But it's my therapist's fault, u know?... He was the one who told me to drink to calm my nerves....Because I tend to be a lil socially anxious sometimes...So that's why I started drinking.

## Hope, novelist, 64, Greenwich Village

I grew up with an unhealthy dose of Catholicism, which gave me extreme guilt, which translated into self-loathing. So I only dated artists, druggies, flakes, until I met Richard. At first I thought he'd be boring. He came from a good family and was stable. Turns out it's nice not being constantly threatened with eviction or the police knocking weekly. It was true love for once....Richard died of cancer 12 years ago. I thought I'd never get over his death....Time heals. I'm truly happy for having experienced what I did with Richard....
You don't want to look back on life and say, "I should've kissed this person or done that." Live life to the fullest....My therapist kept telling me to love myself and I finally started....I've been in a few relationships since Richard, the longest 6 years, all of them dysfunctional....I'm still writing, even though my books have been met with thundering silence....I've loved 3 people in my life; the

other 2 were gay friends who died of AIDS....I tried nonfiction, but it felt boring. I can pour myself into my fictional characters.

## 501-208-XXXX
Have a shot for me.

## Ashley
I'm drunk as a skunk....It poured rain all morning on the metal roof of this mobile home....Only if I get a dick pic from you...Thanks. This new pill I'm on bumped them from 32b to 32c....I'm hammered and driving 66 mph....Ok I'm home alive. You can text me without guilt....I mean I miss you too!... I'm pretty needy when I'm drunk. To be honest...You're adorable....I would fawn all over you right now....Did I tell you already I'm drunk because roofer Jeff stood me up tonight?... He was supposed to meet me at applebees at 7. I waited an hour. Then started downing gin and cranberries....I wish you were here. We would be all over each other. I'd be rubbing your shoulders and you'd be—well, you know....I would watch a video of your jacking off multiple times....Do it......I'd be happy with a pic too....Wine 30 baby!... I'm celebrating. A cruise company allied with *National Geographic* wants me to come for an interview to be an environmental tour guide on their ships...Blue Sky Adventuroo. Look em up....God this sucks. I miss you....You and I are 2 classy motherfuckers. You know that?... Do you know what lovebugs are?... See, I'd be such a cheap easy date....I'm horny. I want to be fucked by you so badly....I would love that right now.

## Woman from Venice
Are you sure? I might look like crap and be jetlagged.

**Erica**

Busy being a craq hoar.

**832-729-XXXX**

I haven't dated in a while, and I'm pretty close to my mom. I'm Tina, by the way.

**224-622-XXXX**

If the ones I've loved had loved me the way I loved them...Life would've been different....I think you want to get to bed....You scare me a little....No, you don't scare me like you think...You scare me because when we text I feel like we already know each other and plus a very good friend.

**Rianna, 25, Tacoma, Washington (253-779-XXXX)**

I can't really talk to my friends about my feelings. I've never cried to a friend. I was an only child, which is lonely, and my mom died of breast cancer when I was 13. My dad was 51 when they had me, and after Mom died I became this wild, insanely depressed teenage girl. Drugs, drinking, sex with randoms. I didn't care. I just wasn't close to my dad. We shared a house, but we didn't talk or know each other. He watched me disintegrating. He didn't know what to do. He was in mourning too. I survived, and the weird thing is, my craziness actually brought me closer to my father. He's 76 now and will be dying soon. He's really the only person I have to talk to. He really did well in life. Self-starter. Nicest guy there is, and I can't stand that he's going to die soon. It's too much....It's amazing you're anonymous...

*Rianna began to cry. I did, too. I really didn't know what to say. I told her she can call anytime. I'd like to know her for the rest of my life, actually. I feel her. I "knew" her before I met her. That type of instant connection. She texted me an hour later: "Thank you Jeff. I would love to remain friends. I will call you again." Rianna is the third call out of thousands I started crying on.*

## Whitney (703-909-XXXX)

That's understandable, I suppose. Mine was just as bad....I moved overseas from him and we thought what we had was strong enough to have a stable, long-distance relationship....We just fought all the time. He didn't make much of an effort. I had an epiphany that he wasn't worth it and all the pain and all the missing weren't worth it. And I got over it....Oh I'm fantabulous. It's been about 2 years since I've seen him....I almost might be dating someone else....But do you think that the fact that you still talk might bring you and Kira back together?

## 201-783-XXXX

Do you ever feel like there is no future? Or present? Well, a moment never lasts. Next thing you know you're in another. You never know what might happen, but whatever it is, time goes on and just after that, the moment's passed. I believe that there is no present and the future always has to be further and further away. If you ever feel that something will take forever to end, just remember that once it's over, you can slip back into the past any time you like.

## 610-999-XXXX

In adolescence we take it for granted. In adulthood it's constant work to even catch a glimpse of happiness. Sometimes it's next-to-impossible. I feel like shit today; sorry for being a downer. Yes, I'm Doris Downer.

## Albert (347-441-XXXX)

Think we'll be lonely forever?... And just find a girlfriend or wife that likes us?... But we will still be alone and just fake our own happiness.

*Jim Caviezel says I need to count my blessings and be happy—be happy I'm not a quadriplegic. He said there are countless happy quadriplegics. Basically, he's saying don't focus on the dark areas of your life. Forgive your parents. Move on. He suggested I read* Left to Tell, *the story of Immaculée Ilibagiza, who survived the Rwandan genocide by hiding in a closet for 91 days. Her entire family was slaughtered.*

## Ashley

Well, that stinks....My sister was born with a congenital heart defect—tricuspid atresia. Her first surgery to correct it was done at a teaching hospital. The intern fucked up the anesthesia toward the end when she came out of surgery at 6 months old. She started moving, dislodged a blood clot, and had a stroke. Nothing could bring back our perfect girl....She has complete left-hand paralysis and cognitive retardation, but she's relatively healthy and happy now....I have no idea what to do with my life. I started college at 15.

Full scholarship. First in my family to go to college. And over the last 6 months all my grandiose visions of what my life would be have shattered....They were the only hospital that accepted our crappy insurance....I can't sleep, sheesh....It's been 5 days since I quit Oxy for the 3rd time. New record. I'm going to reward myself with a pack of Marlboros....Thanks.

### Tamika

We're playing truth or dare. Will you give us a dare jeff?... We usually dare each other to go out on the streets and ask strangers bizarre questions....They usually walk away laughing haha

### Pimp, NYC

You ok?... You know, you're too old to be posting your number on the streets, man....Oh yeah. Gettin' any?... What kind of chick would meet a guy from a street poster?... Listen, I've got a lot of great women for you by the hour.

*I told the pimp I had plenty of women. He laughed and hung up.*

### Ashley

Ha ha. I think I can tell....Lilacs! They smell nice!... I don't have a single pet right now. It makes me so sad....I do not like the life I'm living at all....White zinf will always be my 1st love. *(Picture of a glass of wine on a table.)*...So tired. Up and job hunting again tomorrow at 6 am...Good morning my good fellow....You have lovely ears.... Three part-time jobs landed....If there's one thing I've mastered, it's winning at interviews....I see you deleted your Facebook....How am I supposed to admire your Davidian form now?... Ah...In a coffee shop having espresso. I have another interview at 11....Sleepy already. But in a good book...Just finished a couple online retail apps....Working on my app for the sheriff's office now...I think I'd enjoy that....I miss your intermittent texts during the day too. It's like seeing a bluejay....I miss you too. If it's possible to miss someone you haven't met...A strange thought, isn't it? Well, goodnight my distant smile....Working at this place both brings me to a dark place, by seeing some of the worst of humanity has to offer, but also lifts me up somewhat by the always generous input from the community....How did you know there's nothing I find more desirable than a man who employs a hearty Shakespearean "alas"?

## Bill (616-821-XXXX)

I've never actually seen it, but I looked up Hamlet the Dane on Google and was reading the play and it's hella deep. I dig it. I read Act 5 Scene 1, the part where he says, "What is he whose grief bears such an emphasis, whose phase of sorrow conjures the wandering stars and makes them stand like wonder-wounded hearers?" That is an epic line, man, Hamlet's moody, dark, and ferocious with his words but amazing in general.

> Hamlet says, "I am with more offences at my beck than I have thoughts to put them in, imagination to give them shape, or time to act them in." I'm heavily flawed. One positive feature I have, though, is a self-reflexive nature. I know I've made many mistakes, but I do learn from them. I'm constantly charting what I did wrong—what I did right—and trying to improve. I'm a roving, sloshing work-in-progress.

**Ashley**

That was such a nice book. It's for a bonfire on Friday....I think there's something happening to all of us. We're being engulfed in old emotions and memories and it's almost like we're living in them.

**Cancer survivor, 18, Yonkers, New York (914-318-XXXX)**

My mom had breast cancer and I was diagnosed with ovarian cancer at 16....I did my chemo at Sloan Kettering. The worst thing is I hated how I lost all my strength....Thank you. So far I'm cancer free....I got accepted to NYU!

**720-984-XXXX**

Lame ass school, urf, then i worked on a big project and now im on my way to the dentist.

**Ashley**

I relapsed. Damn...I just got fired for sleeping on the job....I guess it isn't the end of the world. It was a crazy demanding job. And I never quite fit in with the rest of the highly religious evangelical staff. That may have been part of it....Fuckfuckfuck. I'm freaking out. I keep driving in circles around the block....The only goddamn job around here I could get and I blew it. Now I have $1200 to my name....I refuse to cry. Maybe I'll just drive away and never come back.

**Scott, 33, Wisconsin (920-784-XXXX)**

Two nights before I got sober, the drive to kill myself was so massive, so monumental that I had the shotgun to my mouth....I was broken enough inside to ask for help....Thanks......Sober 41 months. First year I felt like I was all over the place because I've never been sober as an adult. I even danced sober; that was a trip, bud....I try to live by the Albert Camus idea of getting the most experience out of the time you have....I'm not perfect by any means, but I'm satisfied with my life....Be honest with yourself, don't twist yourself around, see through the traps of life, the pitfalls.

## 785-383-XXXX

But I kinda need to vent. Two days ago my dad tried to commit suicide. He drank a gallon of antifreeze....His veins are collapsing and his lungs are doing this shit. It's the 9th time....But I don't want him to fucking die. And he probably will....Retaining water... My family yelled at me when I threatened to take him to the hospital. They told me if he wants to die, let him....They are tired of him.

## 779-221-XXXX

I walked around downtown, hoping to meet people and go with the flow, but it wasn't fun.

## 619-594-XXXX

Excited to have ya, Jeff. We're near the border, where all the drugs get smuggled in.

## Ashley

Hey, I ain't walkin' no straight and narrow either, brother.

## Kimberly

I know you're not like this. Are you just trying to drive me away?

## Melicent (646-673-XXXX)

Apparently there's going to be a lunar eclipse tonight....I'm going to some Christmas party with my husband at his company but I just came back from hanging with the whitest kids I know. We were jamming to Missy Elliot....You're lucky you're going out. I'm about to go to some bullshit Christmas party.

## Lynda (908-420-XXXX)

My crippling alcoholism made most of my friends abandon me. I was in a 4-year relationship and was cheated on, and then a year-long relationship and he fell out of love with me. My most recent relationship was 3 years ago....I'm lonely too. Sorry to hear about your breakup....It gets better. However, again, a lot of healing is time. Just gotta find ways to not think about it and burn steam off.

## Erica

I sit in my apartment and stare at these balls of gas every night. Hoping for something new, wanting to go up there, view galaxies. But these stars, they're just fucking balls of gas that eventually fade away, burning like embers. No one remembers them, and the ones who do, they eventually die along with them, and they both fade away in memory. That's me, Jeff. I'm the burning ball of gas.

## 618-447-XXXX

Too lazy. And I don't know how to turn it up. It's not my house!... Lying in bed, freeeeeeezing!

## 347-858-XXXX

Fighting a fever! Otherwise great.

**Melody**

I hear that...I guess that can be good or bad.

**480-712-XXXX**

Uninteresting, but good. Too bad nothing cool ever happens to me. How are you?

**Brittany**

Not very good actually...Just life shit...Left my parents' house a few weeks ago. Living with a friend instead.

> *Brittany sent a picture of a skeleton screwing a woman with text: "Creepy picture of a skeleton having sex with a naked girl on the wall of the restaurant we ate at."*

**646-483-XXXX**

what's ur tombstone gonna say? how u be remembered?

**Brittany**

You really think I'd send pictures of myself and then refuse to have sex with you?

**Art (561-838-XXXX)**

And I just realized how creepy this text probably looks....I under-stand the loneliness, Jeff. Hang in there....I swear I'm normal. Well, as normal as one can be!

> *Caitlin, a Texas college student I've texted with a few times, called, and we talked for two hours. The awkward pauses*

*didn't matter. We were comfortable. She's extremely nice and sounds identical to Juliette Lewis. Says her boyfriend's a nerd. Hates going to comic-book stores with him, but that's required. She says they smoke a lot of weed and watch movies. Somehow sex got brought up, and she said that women talk just as raunchily as men. Most of her female friends watch porn. She isn't too into it, though. Prefers going to music festivals. I asked if, living in Texas, she has to stay out of the sun a lot. She laughed and said she's black, but she, too, gets sunburned. Recently bought a kite and loves flying it. Looking up at the sky, she feels calm. She fears that a degenerative brain disorder is beginning to afflict her. Caitlin also thinks/hopes it's just from smoking too much weed. She loves indie films, recommends* Blue Valentine.

## Lilly (678-314-XXXX)

Do you enjoy talking to me? I feel like I know nothing about you. And vice versa...Regardless, you are still a friend to me.

## Billie

You're just saying that....How and where would you touch me?... Because I'm really fat....I'm not sexy....Would you caress me?... Would you be gentle with me?... You wouldn't. I have this really weird claw-shaped birthmark on my shoulder and it's disgusting.... No you don't....You're just saying that....I'd really like you to kiss me, though....Thank you. I'm not, though, Jeff....I hope we kiss sometime soon. I want you....I don't see why, though....I'm so imperfect and confused. And you're wonderful.

## 917-361-XXXX

Aww, I wish someone felt like that about me. Kira was lucky.

## Same person sending same text over and over

Forever alone...Forever alone...Forever alone...

## 347-376-XXXX

You seem nice!... Really bored...Like what? What kind of mistakes?

## Lacey

Hi Jeff. Results positive, you are indeed the father.

## Krystal

Can I start calling you Dad?... Fine. You win. We won't talk about sex cuz I'm 17. But I think your rule is dumb.

## Jermaine

I committed my first theft last night....A watch from Belk.

## 201-783-XXXX

Do you think if humans never closed their hands, Jeff, we wouldn't have creases on our palms?

## 276-870-XXXX

I went to my first Black Friday with a friend for the hell of it. Didn't buy anything. Just helped her carry her stuff, and I stole a necklace. I cut off the sensor with my pocketknife and left it on my wrist....Part of me feels justified. Like it was a social rebellion against consumerism and corporations....It's the most expensive piece I have now.

**Tad**

Do you play mind games?

**Restricted-number man**

My best friend's mother just died. He wants to commit suicide. What do I do?

*I told this man that he must get professional help immedi-ately for his friend. Do not mess around with it. Get him to a hospital or dial 911. Do not have any amateurs deal with the situation. Professional help only.*

**Jordan**

At a party I was slipped something and eventually I like passed out on my stomach in bed. But when I woke up the next day someone had Superman-ed me.... *(I ask her what that means.)*....Superman-ing is when a guy cums on a girl's upper back when she's passed out. He sticks the sheets on the cum and smears it around and leaves the sheets on her so that in the morning the sheets are stuck to her, like a cape, and it's a pain to get off.

**Don, 39, Queens**

You are a noble man, Lonely Jeff. Much stronger than I am. Which nearly begs the question, why are you lonely? You deserve an award, Bold Boy.

**646-460-XXXX**

Do you even know my name?

**Jermaine**

The media makes Hollywood glamorous, but in fact it's dirty and full of bums. I've never seen a star in Hollywood. The media acts as if stars are walking around everywhere. Negative. I saw Adam Sandler in a supermarket. He looked sad.

*I was looking around this room, thinking about how much I hate my life. I'm at the point where I should probably stay away from Kira for good. She must sense this. Her reasoning is that I need to be her friend right now because she has a severe kidney infection. She keeps saying she could die. I think she's sick but not going to die. I think she's just lonely.*

**Kimberly**

Hey! You're totally gonna stay and talk to me....That's so weird. I never thought this was illegal....So you can't talk with me because I'm 17?... Then I won't talk about sex.

**970-846-XXXX**

You are a criminal mastermind, Mister Jeff. My hero. The George Washington of the underbelly. If you weren't so morally corrupt, I'd fly there and fuck ya. But I don't want herpes again.

**Restricted-number man**

I have a white shirt on. I order chocolate ice cream, walked out, someone bumps into me, and now my shirt is brown. What do I do?

*I told restricted-number man to go change his shirt. Don't get mad. It was an accident.*

**Claude, 50, Brooklyn**

Hey, Jeffrey. This situation actually presented itself to the writer Paul Auster, who was on a flight to Paris. He went to use the restroom. An exceptionally attractive French woman comes out of the restroom, smiling. Paul goes in the restroom and sees a humongous turd on the closed toilet lid. Would you get the airline stewardess and explain what happened, thinking there's a chance she might not believe you? The stewardess could think you're a sicko and into toilet tricks. Or would you—I think the term today is "man up"—clean up this woman's mess?

**215-401-XXXX**

Sorry, it's not going to work out, but I have a friend and you look exactly like her type. Her name is Lilyane and her number is 908-385-XXXX. Good luck.

**Krystal**

You're going to find a girl to take care of your needs. Then you will forget me....I may be 17, but I know how the world works, buster.

**Amanda, works in marketing**

Two of my closet friends are extremely passive-aggressive. Neither will be open with the other. What should I do?... Better people will move into your life after a breakup....I lost my father when I was 9. I have a fear of abandonment....You've helped people by sharing your loneliness....I grew up in a family that didn't talk about feelings. We toughed it out....I recommend Estancia 460. It's a very warm, welcoming, and happy restaurant in TriBeCa.

## Miles, 51, Indianapolis (317-828-XXXX)

It's this place for guys to get their hair cut called Sports Clips. Like a locker room with TVs everywhere. I'm a bargain shopper and got a coupon for it. So I'm really excited the first time I'm there. A beautiful brunette with cleavage for days came out to get a customer. I was like, this is great. Another hot blonde came out to get another guy. When they called my name I got the big old ugly wench.

## Elissa (206-816-XXXX)

She scared off black bears while I would hike, but she was scared of water.

## 352-406-XXXX

Aw cute! Water dogs are so fluffy!... What do I want out of life? Happiness. And to make others happy...Peace. The Beatles. Twizzlers...I'm having one of those nights where I'm feeling extremely sorry for myself....What do you want?

## 252-955-XXXX

Sweet dreams but don't let the bed bunnies bite.

## Katrina

Hey someone changed the names in my phone—who's this?... Who?... Who's the lonely guy?... Oh, you got changed to God.

## Girl, NYU student (440-935-XXXX)

I need god-blood, jesus juice—coffee...I have to get up now.

**928-300-XXXX**

I drink a lot of coffee in class. I put John the Coffee, instead of John the Baptist, on an exam. Oops.

**309-235-XXXX**

Still awake jeff?

*First date tonight with Paige. We walked through Central Park and had espresso. Vibrant chemistry. She's 23, a Columbia grad, exquisite green eyes, a painter, and an excellent conversationalist with a gorgeous body. First thing she said to me when I complimented her pink coat was, "It's much better underneath." Indeed. We're going to the De Kooning exhibit at MOMA. Paige's mom is dead set against her going out with "Jeff, one lonely guy." I don't blame her. Paige is yet another girl with an eating disorder I've met through this flyer. She says it's much more complex than trying to keep her weight down. Among other things, "it's very much about addiction." She can't stop drinking when she starts. She's passed out on the street a couple times. Made many "bad barroom decisions, like who I've gone home with. A long list of undesirables."*

**224-381-XXXX**

I doubt I'll be able to sleep, though...Transformers 3...I generally watch the same movie every night, and this isn't the same movie.

**Girl, NYU student (440-935-XXXX)**

That's interesting…Why do you think I'm ambivalent?… I have definitely changed opinions on things too. I used to think a lot differently about people and life. I thought people could change and be helped. But not so much at all now…I don't believe it.

**715-771-XXXX**

What more can we do?… We can't just show up naked, can we?… There is little to be done beyond that.

*I think of the experiment I read about recently: a man walked through the streets of Manhattan, stopping complete strangers to ask them, very sincerely, "Are you ok?" Apparently many of them began crying on the spot.*

# About the Authors

**Jeff Ragsdale** has worked as stand-up comedian, actor, and home builder. He lives in New York City.

**David Shields** is the author of 11 previous books, including *Reality Hunger: A Manifesto*, named one of the best books of 2010 by more than 30 publications, and *The Thing About Life Is That One Day You'll Be Dead*, a *New York Times* bestseller. His work has been translated into 15 languages.

This is **Michael Logan**'s first book. Excerpts from his book-in-progress, a work of nonfiction, have appeared in *Conjunctions*.